Iraq, the Gulf States
&
the War

a changing relationship
1980–1986
and beyond

Gerd Nonneman

Ithaca Press
London & Atlantic Highlands
1986

For my parents

Eduard and Aldegonde Nonneman

Exeter Middle East Politics Series   No1
Series Editor: Tim Niblock

© 1986 Gerd Nonneman

First published in 1986 by
Ithaca Press
13 Southwark Street   London SE1 1RQ
&
171 First Avenue   Atlantic Highlands NJ 07716
Printed and bound in England by
Biddles Ltd   Guildford & King's Lynn

ISBN   0 86372 073 0   paperback
ISBN   0 86372 078 1   cased

TABLE OF CONTENTS

SERIES EDITOR'S PREFACE

This is the first book to be published in the Exeter
Middle East Politics Series. Gerd Nonneman's work began
as a dissertation written in partial fulfilment of the
requirements for his MA degree at the University of
Exeter. The substantial documentation which he has
accumulated on a highly critical subject - and one that
has received very little attention elsewhere - fully
merits in my opinion rushing this work to early
publication. Nonneman demonstrates convincingly that
Iraq's relations with the Gulf states both affect Iraq's
ability to wage war and impinge on the character and form
of Iraqi foreign policy in general. The future of the
Gulf states themselves will be shaped by the policies
they have pursued and the relationships they have
maintained during the war. Hence the significance of
Nonneman's well-researched work.

The writer's personal experience in the area, and his
ability to use Arabic-language material, have given him
considerable insight into the political and economic
processes which have shaped developments.

Tim Niblock
University of Exeter

PREFACE

Many people who helped me wish to remain anonymous; my thanks to them are no less fulsome for that. My greatest debt,however, is to Dr. Tim Niblock of Exeter University, my academic 'mentor' in the full literal meaning of that word. Dr. Niblock was as supportive and encouraging as he was painstaking in his criticism - without all of which this work would never have reached its present standard. In addition, special thanks must go to Jonathan Crusoe of **MEED**, for letting me partake of his valuable experience and for the time and effort spent in trying to find some pieces to fit the puzzle; Simon Henderson, of **MidEast Markets**; Dr. Keith McLachlan, of the School for Oriental and African Studies; and Dr. George Joffe, of the **Economist Intelligence Unit.** I am grateful, also, to the academic and other staff at the Centre for Arab Gulf Studies at the University of Exeter, for clearing away some hurdles and making others easier, in fact almost pleasant to take. All the other helping hands who provided me with their impressions and sometimes a further piece of the puzzle, will not blame me for abstaining from listing them here. They know, I trust, that they have my appreciation.

If any errors in fact and judgement remain, it is in spite of all this help: responsibility for those is solely my own.

INTRODUCTION

A lot of effort has been spent in writing about the now almost six years-old Gulf War between Iran and Iraq, and much speculation has ensued about the effect of the war on political relations in the Arab Gulf. Little research into the latter topic, however, has been done. In the present volume therefore, the writer intends to consider in detail how the war has affected the development of relations between .Iraq and the six Arab Gulf states – relations which had been unfolding since the mid-1970s – and whether the behaviour of both sides consisted merely of ad hoc reactions to the situations prevailing, or on the contrary had long-term implications.

The first chapter looks at the pre-war development of relations and their determinants, in the framework of the over-all evolution of these countries' foreign policies. For the purposes of this study, the war has been divided into six periods (see Appendix II). In chapters II - VII, the political relations and attitudes which developed in each of those periods will be analysed. An eighth chapter covers the evolution of socio-economic relations since the war, not only because of their intrinsic importance as a part of Iraqi-Arab Gulf relations, but also because, as will be shown, they have long-term implications for the general state of relations.

Statistical material about Iraqi-Arab Gulf trade and about the financial position of the seven states under consideration, as well as a list of high-level visits between Iraq and the Six, and some further documents, are presented in Appendices and form an integral part of the work.

Work on this study has meant having to piece together what was rather like a puzzle; building up, on the basis of published evidence, official sources, confidential information and 'rumours', a composite picture with reference to which the meaning and reliability of new elements of information could be assessed. The writer also draws on his impressions while living in Iraq and travelling in the Gulf , 1982 - 1984, and from discussions with people in banking, academic and journalistic circles. The picture was further complemented by information and impressions collected while in the Gulf states in the period leading up to, during and after the February 1986 Iranian offensive.

CHAPTER ONE

THE PRE-WAR BACKGROUND

A. IRAQI FOREIGN POLICY : THE FRAMEWORK

1. The orientation and evolution of Iraqi foreign policy

In the Report of the 8th Regional Congress of the Baath
Party in Iraq, four "basic considerations" are enumerated
as underlying the Party's foreign policy:

1. The requirements of the Arab liberation
struggle and its main issues, especially those of
Palestine and the Gulf.

2. The need to protect the Revolution in Iraq as a
fighting base for the movement of Arab Revolution
in pursuit of its objectives of Unity, liberty and
socialism.

3. The belief that the Arab Revolution is an
integral part of world revolution, with which we
must ally ourselves in the struggle against
imperialism, aggression, plunder and racial
discrimination,... but at the same time taking
every care, theoretical and practical, to
safeguard the independence and distinctive
features of the Arab revolution.

4. Belief in the need to establish friendly
relations between the Arab people and the states
of the world, in accordance with our domestic and
Pan-Arab interests and with the principles of
brotherhood and co-operation between peoples. (1)

Pan-Arab nationalism has always been a major component of
Baath ideology. The socialist and revolutionary
components of the ideology, however, were generally
stressed under al-Bakr who accepted the need for
closer ties with the Soviet Union. Hence, as KASHKETT
points out, the isolation of Iraq from mainstream Arab
politics (2). It was Pan-Arabism and "the independence

and distinctive features of the Arab revolution", which
from the mid-1970s gained in comparative weight, as, we
would suggest, Saddam's domination of the formulation of
ideology and decision-making grew into a monopoly (3).
Indeed, over the following years one sees a definite
evolution in the Baath position - which is, incidentally,
almost invariably put forward by Saddam. In 1975 he
outlined his understanding of the international system as
one developing from a bi-polar into a multi-polar system
by 1995. In such a system, Iraq would get more room for
manoeuvre; it should use the configuration of power to
the advancement of the Arab Nation, making possible a
true political independence (4). Indeed, non-alignment
for Saddam is not only desirable in itself, but
constitutes the only sensible way of handling this
changing global system (5).

The change in stress from 1974 (explicitly) and the role
of the then vice-chairman of the RCC in that change
(implicitly) are confirmed by Saddam himself in a recent
interview with Egyptian journalists (6). Progressively,
therefore, the central elements in Iraq's foreign policy
orientation became non-alignment and Arab Nationalism.
This could go hand in hand with a more pragmatic approach
to international relations - it was indeed partly
prompted by it - that was also very much an input of
Saddam. Baath ideology remained change-oriented, but the
sequence of the slogan "Unity, Freedom, Socialism"
already opened the way for normalised relations with
'conservative' Arab and other regimes. This pragmatism
was necessary to allow Iraq to assume the more active and
leading role in the Arab and Third World, that Saddam
felt was the country's logical task. The Report of the
9th Regional Congress of the Baath Party in Iraq, in
retrospect, considered Iraq's actual participation in
non-aligned affairs in the mid-1970s insufficient when
compared with its enhanced weight and its principles.
Consequently, the Report notes, the Party actively
searched for ways to give Iraq its logical place in the
movement; hence Saddam's personal participation in the
Havana Conference in 1979. Without being explicit, the
Report also notes that this evolution coincides with
Saddam's formal take-over, and stresses the strong
development in Iraq's participatory activities between
July 1979 and the beginning of the war - and ever since
(7). The 1974 principles quoted above are reaffirmed,
but at the same time, Iraq's greater international
importance and the "development" of its international
relations and economic policies are pointed out (8).
Regarding Iraq's duty to help the Third World and the
Arabs, the stress of earlier periods on the political

aspect (the fight against imperialism), says the Report, had to shift to the economic: since with the world recession and higher energy prices, the main danger for Third World countries has become economic, economic help became the prime necessity (9). This ties in with another important focus of Iraqi foreign policy under Saddam, viz. the building of NIEO, a New International Economic Order (10).

The actual foreign policy behaviour of the Iraqi state is not solely determined by the party line - even the new more flexible party line - as it is described above. In fact, "Saddam Hussein has made the point that it was not necessary to have total congruence between the party's positions and those of the state. ... The state has to adapt to changing circumstances and conduct day-to-day affairs; the party does not" (11). As it is, with Saddam effectively being the main ideologue in the party, the party line has come to include an array of pragmatic attitudes that make it easier to defend elements of Iraqi foreign policy behaviour as ideologically sound.

Thus, Iraqi foreign policy behaviour is determined by three categories of elements. First, the 'pure' Baath ideological orientation, since the mid-1970s progressively dominated by nonalignment and pan-Arab Nationalism. Thus, Soviet activities in the PDRY, Ethiopia, Cambodia and Vietnam were condemned. Relations with the PDRY regime were broken off in late March 1980, because of that regime's strongly pro-Soviet line (and its sheltering of Iraqi communist exiles) and an "opposition front" was set up (12). The invasion of Afghanistan was strongly opposed and undoubtedly accelerated Iraq's shift toward the West. Iraq became a big customer for French arms, particularly in 1980 (13), which meant a break in its traditional dependence on the USSR for arms supplies. The diversification of armament sources would be enshrined in the Report of the 9th Regional Congress of the Baath Party in Iraq, as an essential prerequisite for preserving national independence (14).

Second, pragmatic but ideologically 'sound' considerations. These include the change in attitude so as to allow Iraq to assume its logical leading role in the nonaligned movement and the Arab World, and a shift in the stance on the Palestine question for tactical reasons (15). Strategic and raison d'etat considerations are put forward which justify new policies in terms of "defending the Revolution in Iraq".

Third, a number of domestic motives which help explain
the shift to 'moderation' and towards the West. On the
one hand, having acquired in the wake of the oil price
hikes of 1973-4, enough funds to speed up development at
an unprecedented rate, Iraq needed the West to sell it
the building blocks for that development and for later
imports of consumer goods. These could not be provided by
the Soviet Union. The shift to moderation helped to draw
the West closer(16). The acquired oil wealth also gave
Iraq the financial independence and economic freedom to
choose for a turn to the West. On the other hand, the
improved domestic security of the regime against external
as well as internal plots, meant that it no longer to the
same extent needed a revolutionary posture on account of
which to dismiss rivals and opponents. Moreover, the
regime understandably felt it could gain enormously in
domestic prestige from the enhanced position in the
non-Aligned movement and the Arab world, which it could
only achieve by moderating its policies. Feeling
directly threatened by Iran, Iraq also hoped to gain
assistance from some neighbouring countries - Turkey and
Jordan - to help ease the Iraqi-Iranian tension (17).

The shift began in 1974, gained momentum from 1975, and
was dramatically catalysed by the Baghdad Summit of 1978,
which in the words of one observer, "appears to have
given Iraq a taste for diplomacy" (18). But more recently
yet another factor in Iraq's changing attitude has become
obvious, confirming the observed evolution and giving it
a long-term character: Iraq has adopted, particularly
from 1979, an economic liberalisation policy, implying a
degree of **infitah** and privatisation. SPRINGBORG
convincingly argues that this is at least partly a
reflection of Saddam's efforts to enhance his grip on
power by weakening the hold of the Baath over the economy
through encouragement of the private sector, and thus
"(paving) the way for the emergence of a new, as yet
amorphous group rather than class, upon which an
increasing amount of the President's political base and
legitimacy rest" (19). Earlier, KHAFAJI had already
presented evidence for the existence of an alliance of
the ruling group with the Iraqi commercial bourgeoisie
(20).

The shape of Iraqi foreign policy on the eve of the Gulf
war, therefore, was decidedly different from what it had
been only 6 years before. It crystallised in the
"National Charter" which Saddam put forward on 8 February
1980, proposing that this should be adhered to by all
Arab states (see Appendix I) (21), The Charter stressed
strict non-alignment, peaceful means of solving problems

between Arab states, Arab mutual defense, the adherence
to international law, and Arab economic integration. The
most remarkable element was implicit: there was no
mention of the Arab peoples, only of states.

2. Behaviour towards the Gulf states before the war

Policy and behaviour of the Baath regime in Iraq towards
the Gulf evolved in the frame of the general evolution
of Iraqi foreign policy as outlined above. The main
specifically Gulf-related determinants (22) during the
1968-1980 period have been the stress on non-alignment
and the Arab character of the Gulf (23) (implying the
importance of Iraqi influence) , in interaction with the
Iranian attitude and the response of the Arab Gulf
states. NIBLOCK argues that frictions have been a result
of those interactions, and that Iraq would have wished
good relations with the Arab Gulf states all along. The
non-alignment principle meant trying to lure the Arab
Gulf states away from the West. The principle of the Arab
character of the Gulf and the necessity for an Iraqi role
in the Gulf meant opposition to Iranian (non-Arab)
influence, and, because of the degree of Iranian control
over the Shatt al-Arab, also necessitated some Iraqi
control over the Kuwaiti islands Warba and Bubiyan which
'blocked' the approach to the second Iraqi port Umm Qasr.
The claim on Kuwait had been given up by the 1968 regime.
The two principles were interlinked because Iran was also
an ally of the West.

The six Arab Gulf states, and Saudi Arabia in particular,
stuck to a pro-Western line and moreover preferred Iran
over Iraq as their 'ally' in the regional balance. Hence
Iraq's enmity: as NIBLOCK puts it, "The Ba'th's
'subversive role', in fact, may have been more the effect
than the cause of the problems in Iraq's relations with
the Arab states of the Gulf" (24). Although it would seem
that one can not, as NIBLOCK seems to do, dismiss the
wish for political change as a motive in Iraqi actions in
the Gulf (after all, Baath ideology remained
change-oriented and claimed validity for the whole Arab
world, and Iraq did train guerillas for PFLOAG, whose
horizons were wider than just Oman), it never appears to
have been a major element, losing further in importance
since the general foreign policy shift in 1975 (25).

That shift in general policy had a parallel in regional
affairs, offering a further explanation for Iraq's
changed stance (after all the Gulf was Iraq's immediate

environment and can be assumed to have influenced
Saddam's overall perceptions). The 1975 general shift
coincided roughly with the Algiers Agreement, the further
change in 1978 with the beginning of the Iranian
revolution.

In practical terms, therefore, as far as Iraqi attitudes
to the Arab Gulf states are concerned, the crucial
factors were Iran and the orientation of those states.
There were several dimensions to this. First, strategic,
in that Iranian control over the Shatt (coupled with
Kuwaiti sovereignty over Warba and Bubiyan) jeopardised
Iraq's military capacity in the Gulf. Second, economic,
as the Shatt and the Gulf constituted one of Iraq's main
outlets to the world. Third, ideological: non-Arab and
pro-Western Iran's influence had to be curbed. Fourth,
more broadly political: the Iraqi position and influence
in the region had to be strengthened.

The 1975 agreement with Iran temporarily ended the
perception of that country as a direct rival and a source
of threats. Differences with the Arab Gulf states on this
account thus diminished. Shortly after the agreement was
concluded, there were even discussions of some kind
between the 'big three' regarding regional security,
although this came to nothing. The Iranian revolution of
1978-79 reintroduced the Iranian threat, but this time
the Arab Gulf states felt equally threatened and thus
objectively and subjectively ended up (or remained) in
Iraq's camp. For Iraq, the new configuration also
heightened the need for the building of pro-Iraqi **axes**,
to include all anti-Iranian forces.

In February 1979 a mutual internal security agreement was
signed with Saudi Arabia (for which consultations had
started in April of the previous year (26)). This showed
its effectiveness when in the same year, after seizing
two boats, the Iraqis tipped off the Saudis about
attempts to smuggle arms into Saudi Arabia, by boats from
the Gulf (27). In April of the same year Iraq declared it
would defend Saudi sovereignty against any, including
Soviet, infringement (28). This was broadened on 6
February, 1980, when the Iraqi Information Minister
declared: "Any attack on any of the Arab Gulf states is a
direct aggression against Iraq" (29). There were reports
about security talks with Kuwait (30), though those did
not lead anywhere at this stage. Relations with Kuwait
had warmed considerably already (31), and when Shaikh
Saad al-Abdullah, the Crown Prince, came to Iraq on a
5-day official visit to talk about economic cooperation,
in May 1980, he was received by government and press as

befits a friend of long standing. (32).

Iraqi diplomatic activity further intensified in the period leading up to the war (to be designated as such, with hindsight, since Minister of Information Latif Nasif Jasim, announced on 8 May, that Iraq considered the 1975 border agreement null and void as a result of Iran's violations of the provisions of the agreement (33)). Pro-Iraqi Shaikh Saqr of Ras al-Khaimah was invited to Iraq and was received by Saddam (34); and renewed border demarcation discussions were suggested to (and accepted by) Kuwait in early July (35). Then, of course, there was Saddam's much commented upon surprise visit to Saudi Arabia on 5 August, when he and a top delegation met with King Khalid and Princes Fahd and Saud al-Faysal for talks on "the current situation in the Middle East and the Gulf region". Discreetly, the joint communique focussed on threatening sanctions against states recognizing Israel's annexation of Jerusalem. Even on that subject, however, it is interesting to note that the position on the Palestinian question was very moderate in comparison to earlier Iraqi declarations (36). Reportedly, Saddam also discussed with King Khalid the reviving of the **Arab Industrialisation Organisation** (AOI), the then moribund Arab arms industry venture (37), in which the UAE and Qatar also enjoyed membership (38)). This obviously had more than merely economic implications. A further warming in Iraq's attitude towards Oman (with which it had established diplomatic relations in 1976) was indicated by the reception given to Qays al-Zawawi on his visit in late May, when Iraq is reported to have specifically promised to send troops to Oman if it were attacked by South Yemen (39).

The points of friction or disagreement that remained on the eve of the war, can be explained with reference to the above mentioned determinants. Warba and Bubiyan retained their strategic and economic importance (and Kuwait remained unwilling to share control). Iraq kept opposing any regional 'bloc formation' outside the Arab League (40). And it kept trying to woo the Arab Gulf states away from their de facto alliance with the West.

B. THE FOREIGN POLICY OF SAUDI ARABIA AND THE SMALLER GULF STATES: THE FRAMEWORK.

1. Determinants and orientation of Saudi foreign policy

Saudi foreign policy is shaped by five main, closely interrelated determinants. Firstly, the absolute primacy of national and regime survival; secondly, the close link between foreign policy and domestic affairs:

> For a regime whose legitimacy cannot be taken for granted and therefore must be anchored in meeting the expectations of its population, the misconduct of its foreign policy could be fatal. A loss of control over oil reserves, the inability to defend the territory of the Kingdom, or the mishandling of foreign exchange assets could be devastating for the House of Saud. (41)

More specifically, as a consequence of the way in which the Saudi state was formed, the Al Saud's legitimacy is to a large extent based on its Islamic credentials. This brings out the third determinant: ideology as a legitimising factor. Islam, as PISCATORI (1983) has made clear, has been an important factor in Saudi foreign policy, primarily with a view to maintaining the regime's security. The same argument can be made for the regime's Arab credentials. Both Islam and Arabism are also important in maintaining the international position of Saudi Arabia and its ruling family.

Fourthly, a crucial determinant lies in Saudi Arabia's **weakness**, rather than its more often stressed (financial) strength. Militarily, demographically, and in terms of the level of capabilities of its indigenous population, the country is no match for the other major actors in the Arab and regional Islamic arena; moreover, the source of its wealth, the country's oil installations, are very vulnerable. This basic position of weakness has led to the need for manoeuvering towards a moderate Arab consensus; and to the necessity of keeping open channels to as many actors as possible. Again, this determinant is linked in with the ones mentioned earlier via the imperatives of survival and domestic legitimacy. As QUANDT has put it: "Pushed and pulled in various directions, [the Saudis] will try to find a safe middle ground, a consensus position that will minimise pressures and threats" (42).

Finally, the character of Saudi foreign policy is also

determined by the decision-making process. Power is
centered at the top of the Al Saud. King Faysal was able
to put his very personal stamp on foreign policy; after
his assassination, however, decision-making has become
more diffuse. In addition to King Khalid and subsequently
King Fahd, decisive voices have been those of the senior
princes Abdullah, Sultan and Nayif, each with somewhat
differing backgrounds, views, sympathies, interests and
tactical postures (43). Consultation and consensus are
key words in this context of diffuse foreign policy
responsibility. "When serious policy differences have
arisen, the familiy has gone to great lengths to prevent
internal quarrels from surfacing. Decisions may be
postponed or compromises forged to preserve the facade of
consensus" (44).

**Characteristics of Saudi policy in the Arab and regional
Islamic arena.**
A first characteristic, which is largely explained by the
above, is the secondary place which Islamic and
anti-communist ideology have taken, giving way to raison
d'etat in its domestic and regional dimensions.
Admittedly, prior to 1975,

> (s)ensitive to the existence of radical forces both
> inside and outside the Kingdom, Faisal's intense
> desire to contain, weaken and ultimately eliminate
> these forces continued to shape Saudi policy.
> Nevertheless, in response to signs of moderation
> from the leading progressive regimes, the Saudi
> regime became more flexible (45),

a tendency which was reinforced when in that same period,
after 1975, Crown Prince Fahd became the regime's strong
man - even if not to the extent of controlling foreign
policy. This links in with a second characteristic,
already referred to above, viz. the efforts expended in
keeping open channels to the 'radicals' (Egypt and Syria,
and later Iraq) and even in cooperating with them if
that could lessen intra-Arab tensions and improve the
chances for a moderate consensus. Thirdly, the Saudi
regime has taken care never to move away too far from the
main body of Arab (governmental) opinion, in order not to
lose its capability for mediation and persuasion and thus
to safeguard its external and domestic balancing
potential and security. As a prime example of this, at
the Baghdad Summits of 1978-79 the Saudis eventually gave
in to the majority position which insisted on sanctions
against Egypt. This was preceded by much wavering, and
reportedly went against the wishes of Fahd (46), but by
March 1979 (Baghdad II) at least the rest of the Saudi

leadership had decided they could not afford to break with the powerful alliance of Iraq, Syria and the rejectionists. A fourth characteristic has been the use of the country's massive funds where this could help smooth relations, reduce radical stands (or over-dependence on the USSR), and generally help build the sought-after moderate consensus which is the only climate in which the Al Saud feel secure.

Fifthly, in virtue of its Islamic credentials, Saudi Arabia has tried to maintain good relations with all the major Islamic countries, including Iran after the revolution. Indeed, both King Khalid and Prince Abdullah in 1979 made it clear they felt that close relations between the Kingdom and the Islamic Republic were possible and desirable, and Iranian verbal attacks were initially played down by the Saudi regime (47). However, when they subsequently came to the conclusion that the Iranian regime had become a real threat to stability and security in the region, not to be subdued by concili- atory gestures, some assertative reaction, using Islamic symbols, became justified; moreover, extra Islamic credit could be acquired by a strong Saudi stance on the questions of Jerusalem and Afghanistan.

Finally, Saudi foreign policy , due to the nature of the decision-making process, has often suffered from indecisiveness, putting off or avoiding of difficult decisions. In QUANDT's assessment, there has been a tendency to panic in crisis situations which would require systematic contingency planning – a requirement "almost antithetical to the Saudi style" (48). A related result has been some degree of inconsistency in Saudi foreign policies. Still the main ingredients are fairly clear, and, as we will argue throughout the rest of this volume, even in the crisis situation of the Iranian threat and the Gulf war, Saudi policy was basically consistent, even if 'frayed round the edges' due to conflicting pressures.

2. Foreign policy determinants in the smaller Gulf states

The foreign policies of the smaller Gulf states are determined (1) by their very smallness, and resulting weakness; and (2) because of this, by their immediate regional environment. None of them can escape the implications which their location in and around the vital oil production and shipping region of the Gulf has for bigger powers; their utter vulnerability only serves to increase this realisation. This can, however, take

different shapes, as witnessed by the diverging
international stances of Kuwait on one extreme and Oman
on the other. In Oman, virtually locked away from the
rest of the Arab world until some fifteen years ago, Arab
nationalism does not have the same legitimising force as
elsewhere; and by virtue of its strategic position, the
country knows it can count on American and western
protection. The Sultan's British military education
provides an additional factor. Still, because of regional
security and economic concerns, Oman has felt the need to
maintain bridges to the moderate Arab majority and in
particular to the other five Arab Gulf states. Kuwait, on
the other hand, is characterised by (1) its position next
to Iraq; and (2) a relatively more politically articulate
population. Both of these elements led it to adopt more
clearly Arab nationalist stands and a more genuinely
non-aligned foreign policy, in order to preserve its
national independence and the regime's domestic
legitimacy. The other Emirates occupy a middle position.
None of the five states can afford to ignore neighbouring
Iran (in part due to their sizable Shi'i population),
nor Iraq (partly because of the salience of Arab
nationalism as a legitimising factor). All, of course,
are influenced by Saudi Arabia.

3. Attitudes of the Arab Gulf states towards Iraq, before the war

In the attitudes of the Arab Gulf States towards Iraq
during the second half of the 1970s, one observes a
legacy of the distrust, opposition (Saudi Arabia) and/or
fear which had built up in earlier periods. This stemmed
from the 1961 Iraqi claim on Kuwait, the border clashes
with Kuwait of 1973 and 1976, and the no doubt partly
justified perception of Iraq as carrying out subversive
activities in those states (see above). But, particularly
after 1975, the Arab Gulf states did show themselves
ready to enter into economic cooperation with Iraq,
although the political dimension lagged behind (49).

In the case of Saudi Arabia, there was an inter-play
between the opening-up of Iraqi foreign policy described
earlier, the Saudi desire to respond to any such
outstretched hand, and the growing pragmatism of Saudi
policy under the influence of Crown Prince Fahd. Only two
days after King Faysal's death, Fahd, in a speech
outlining Saudi policy, expressed the Kingdom's desire
"to cultivate brotherly relations with Iraq" (50). Iraq
was eager enough to respond, but some wariness remained;
the two countries still competed for influence over the

small Gulf states (51). Improved relations with Iraq
provided Saudi Arabia with a welcome counterweight
against Iran. When, moreover, Iraq seemed, after Camp
David, to be on its way to capture if not the leadership,
at least a crucial role in Arab politics, the Saudis had
an even stronger incentive for being on good terms with
their Baathist neighbour.

Iraq's bid for regional leadership was partly inspired by
the chaos in Iran after the revolution in 1978 and 1979.
But the rumblings of the Iranian Revolution were also
more directly responsible for a further improvement in
Iraqi-Arab Gulf relations: both the Gulf states and Iraq
now had a similar perception of the threat and an
alliance with Iran was no longer an option. A further
role in the Gulf States' changing attitude towards Iraq
was played by that country's general moderation as
emphasised at the Baghdad Summit, and its growing
coolness towards the USSR, which became very explicit
after the invasion of Afhganistan in 1979. The invasion
also directly influenced the Gulf states' view of
regional security: one Gulf official was quoted as saying
that it had made Iraq "the second line of defence for
protecting the region's oil-producing areas" (52). This
change was manifested in the above-mentioned discussions
and resulting agreement on security, between Iraq and
Saudi Arabia (53), the consultations between Kuwait,
Saudi Arabia and Iraq over ways to keep the Gulf area
free of foreign intervention (54), and the 2-day visit to
Iraq of Bahrain's Crown Prince and Minister of Defence
Shaikh Hamad bin Isa (55). All of the Gulf states except
Oman, moreover, quickly expressed support for the
"National Charter" which Saddam had proposed. Contrary to
SAFRAN's claim that Saudi Arabia did not make its support
explicit for fear of antagonising Syria and Iran (56),
the Kingdom did in fact take a clear stand. King Khalid
declared that

> the announcement of the principles of the charter
> has left the best possible impression on us because
> they are compatible with the policy of
> strengthening the Arab and Islamic position and of
> reinforcing security and stability in the Arab
> homeland. (57)

But at the same time, confidence clearly was not
completely restored and in some ways Iraq was kept at
arm's length. Thus, King Khalid invited his five
fellow-monarchs to attend the Saudi military manoeuvres
at Khamis Mushait, three months after the fall of the
Shah, but not the Iraqi president (58).

In the period leading up to the war, the position of the
Arab Gulf states shifted further - understandably so, in
the light of Bani Sadr's declaration, reported in the
Kuwaiti **Al-Ra'y al-'Amm** (59), that "the Arab governments
in the Gulf area are friends of the US; therefore we do
not consider these states as independent, nor do we wish
to cooperate with them, and Iran intends to export its
Islamic revolution in support of any Islamic movement
that rises against any Arab government (**hukm**)". The
reader may refer to Appendix III for a clear impression
of the increased diplomatic activity by the Gulf regimes
from May 1980 onwards. There was even a visit to Baghdad
by the Omani Minister of Foreign Affairs, Qays al-Zawawi,
who brought a letter from Qabus to Saddam (60). Salalah
radio reported Zawawi as saying on arrival that Oman
wished to initiate cooperation with Iraq and "to remove
any misunderstanding that might have arisen as a result
of certain political opinions" (61). Zawawi supported
Saddam's "National Charter", although he later claimed
that he wanted it clarified and that there was no radical
change in Oman's policy (62). Oman reportedly agreed to
halt talks on a US request for military bases, "in
exchange for development aid and a pledge of military
protection" (63) (Eventually, however, the Americans did
obtain their military facilities). In contrast to the
rest, no Qatari visits to Iraq were recorded, but this
may merely indicate that the Qataris were 'represented'
by the Saudis.

Governmental and press attitudes in the Arab Gulf states
had become decidedly more pro-Iraqi than before. When the
Iraqi-Iranian tension began heating up in April 1980,
leading articles in Gulf newspapers warned Iran not to
venture too far, and at the same time declared solidarity
with Iraq. The Bahraini government firmly put down an
anti-Iraqi demonstration (64), and Prime Minister Shaikh
Khalifa on his early September visit to Iraq was quoted
by Baghdad radio as saying: "Iraq's strength constitutes
strength for all of us and a bulwark for our fateful
course" (65). The Kuwaiti Crown Prince during his May
visit again expressed strong support for Saddam's
"National Charter" and declared that Kuwait joined Iraq
"in any step it takes to preserve Arab achievements and
recover usurped land" (66). Shaikh Saqr of Ras al-Khaimah
when visiting Iraq on 2 June, lauded Iraq's stand on the
Abu Musa and Tunb islands (67), and seemed to support
Iraq's abrogation of the Algiers agreement. He told
reporters that Saddam had informed him about the decision
before delivering the official speech (68). The wording
of the Saudi-Iraqi communique in August also showed

considerable agreement, not only on Palestine but on "the present situation ... in the Islamic world" (which generally indicates relations with Iran), and on "Arab solidarity" (69).

That leaves us with the question whether the Gulf states knew about Iraq's decision to go to war and if so, whether they supported it. There can be no unequivocal answer, but JANSEN's reasons for considering pre-war consultation between Iraq and the Gulf states "scarcely credible" (70) do not seem convincing (Saddam being "a secretive operator by nature"; JANSEN says it would have been "a massive breach of security" to consult the Gulf governments; the Saudis, he claims, would never have agreed - an opinion in which he is followed by PETERSON (71)). In fact, in the regional situation on the eve of the Gulf war it would have been perfectly understandable for the Gulf states to want 'something to be done' about the Iranian threat, not least for the Saudis because of fears of Iranian subversion during the Hajj in October (72). Moreover, the opportunity was certainly the 'least bad' that had presented itself so far, and everything pointed to the probability of a quick Iraqi victory in the case of war. WRIGHT claims that "Iraq agreed with its allies that only after all efforts to negotiate with Iran had been exhausted would it strike ... militarily. Even then, Iraq undertook to limit military action while offering negotiations" (73). Saudi Arabia's position was, she says, one of public "benevolent acquiescence" but privately "more active support covering a range of requests in the event of a war with Iran" (support which, WRIGHT points out, was expressed publicly by "the Saudis' acknowledged spokesmen in the Gulf, the Qataris")(74). Other usually well-informed sources in Saudi Arabia also claimed that that government was fully behind the Iraqi offensive, and AMOS goes along unreservedly with that view, stating that (in addition to King Hussein, King Hassan and Giscard d'Estaing) "the heads of a number of Gulf states" had been informed (75).

Particularly in the case of the Saudis, this putative support for the Iraqi initiative may seem surprising: it may at first sight appear contrary to the indecisiveness and avoidance of critical issues characteristic of Saudi foreign policy, as well as to the Saudi tendency to stay on safe ground. However, the potential for influencing the Iranian government (now clearly an adversary) by shows of good-will appeared exhausted, the balancing act no longer worked, and the imperative of stability and security in this case pressed for action against the Iranian threat. Iran was not thought to be

able put up a serious battle, and an Iraq which would
emerge even stronger than before was still the lesser of
two evils. In this light, SAFRAN's assessment in his
recent study of the Saudis' "quest for Security", viz.
that they came to accept Iraq's military option in
mid-1980, seems plausible (76). Further indications of
their agreement would appear to be provided by the
meeting in August; by the fact that no denial was issued
when Iraq claimed to have obtained the support of all the
Arabian Peninsula states (except the PDRY), after envoys
had explained the government's plans upon the abrogation
of the Algiers agreement on 17 September (77); and by
reactions after the 22 September offensive (see Chapter
II).

C. THE ECONOMIC AND SOCIO-CULTURAL ASPECTS OF RELATIONS BETWEEN IRAQ AND THE ARAB GULF STATES BEFORE THE WAR

As mentioned, the economic aspect of relations became
increasingly important after 1975, reflecting both the
warmer attitude of the Gulf states and the stress placed
by Saddam on interlinking the Arab economies as a
prerequisite for, and a way to bring about, political
unity (78). It led to a structurally higher level of
relations, both governmental and private, and was
accompanied by the improvement of physical infrastructure
linking Iraq to the six. As the development of economic
relations has been admirably treated by SAKR (79), we do
not need to expand on it much here. Iraq was a
participant in a whole range of pan-Gulf
organisations, ministerial conferences and joint projects
in the agricultural, industrial, educational, service,
banking, health, information and cultural sectors, and in
the field of social and labour affairs. The country held
talks on economic cooperation with most Arab Gulf states,
but trade remained on the whole low (see Appendix IV). It
is interesting to note, however, that the Conference of
Planning Ministers held in June 1979 in Riyadh, was
labelled "of the Arabian Peninsula", leaving out Iraq
(80).

Only a few points for comment remain. First, towards the
end of this period, there was increased involvement of
mainly Kuwaiti contracting and trading companies in the
Iraqi market. One non-Kuwaiti example of Gulf private
capital involvement was a $ 135 mn irrigation contract
which went to a Bahrain-based company (81). Secondly, in
the wake of Shaikh Saad's visit to Baghdad in May 1980,
the projects involving the piping of water from the Shatt

al-Arab to Kuwait, and the linking of the two countries'
electricity grids, were revived (82). Thirdly, due to
congestion at the ports of Basra and Umm Qasr, Kuwait's
importance as a transit port for Iraqi goods increased
dramatically.   In 1979, Kuwait agreed to give Iraq-bound
ships access to Mina Shuwaikh (83), and in May 1980
allocated 4 berths (2 at Shuwaykh, 2 at Shuaiba)
exclusively for ships with Iraq-bound cargo (84). UAE
ports too were used for transshipment, and in August 1980
Iraq signed a special agreement with Sharjah for that
purpose (85).

As will have become clear from the above, it was
particularly Kuwaiti-Iraqi economic relations which
expanded dramatically. It was also with Kuwait that the
possibility of a Gulf rail-link was first discussed (86).

Finally, the coordination in oil pricing merits mention:
Iraq in the late 1970s clearly moved towards a more
moderate position in this sphere. During 1980, the
country appears to have coordinated its pricing policy
with the other Gulf states on several occasions (86).

NOTES TO CHAPTER I

1. The 1968 Revolution..., p. 135

2. See KASHKETT, 1982, p. 478

3. MUGHISUDDIN suggests the existence of two main camps:
the civilian ideological hardliners, and the pragmatic
military, Al-Bakr being with the latter. In his
assessment, "Saddam Hussein, though the most influential
leader of the civilian faction, is not in full agreement
with the civilian "hardliners" on such issues as
relations with the Arab states", and on viewing the PLO
as the sole representative of the Palestinians. In fact,
MUGHISUDDIN quotes a report to the effect that Saddam was
in favour of establishing closer relations with Egypt
(whose ties with Saudi Arabia and Iran seemed to worry
Iraqi policy makers): in 1974 the Iraqi government lent
Egypt $ 700 mn, at the initiative of the military faction
supported by Saddam against the "hardliners". Also,
Saddam seems to have tried to dissociate himself from the
supporters of the "rejection front": he is reported to
have told Khaled Fahoum in 1974 that Iraq's policies
towards the Palestinian guerilla organisations would
change, presumably in fvour of the PLO, and that Iraq
would no longer oppose the creation of a Palestinian
state on territory evacuated by Israel. Obviously he did
not have his way then, or did not want to push the matter
for fear of disrupting the Baath. (MUGHISUDDIN, 1977, p.
128).

4. HUSSEIN, 1979, pp. 63 - 84

5. See his speech at the Havana Conference, Sept. 1979,
in **HUSSAIN**, 1981, pp. 131-149; and AHMAD, 1984, p. 158.

6. **Waqa'i'** ..., 1985, pp. 17-18.   The evolution of the
decision making system in Iraq has been such that the
person of Saddam Hussein could indeed come to dominate
the whole process: "From Gang to Elite" (FAROUK-SLUGLETT
& SLUGLETT, 1985) may be an exaggerated description of
that evolution, but the achievement of power was always
linked to personal relationships; since the purges in
1979, power has been completely concentrated in the hands
of Saddam and a few trusted lieutenants.

7. **HIZB**...,1983, pp. 357-358

8. ibid., p. 355

9. ibid., p. 358

10. See AHMAD, 1984, p. 158

11. ibid., p. 159

12. DAWISHA, 1980, p. 138. and (**MEED**, 15-8-80, p. 11)

13. **MEED**, 15-8-80, p. 11: "some 360 TOW anti-tank weapons, 100 AMX-30 tanks and 36 Mirage fighters are on order as well as Italian warships".

14. HIZB..., 1983, pp. 48-49

15. See **Muhandisun tahta tajriba**, a 1977 speech by Saddam, in HUSSAIN, 1981, pp. 73-87.

16. US firms were invited for the first time to take part in the Baghdad International Trade Fair, 1-15 October 1980 (**MEED**, 19-9-80, p. 64).

17. This point is made by KASHKETT, 1982. pp. 484 - 486.

18. DAWISHA, 1980, p. 147 : "Iraq had a great stake in insuring the success of the Conference, but realised at an early stage the difficulties involved in reaching a position acceptable to all Arab states ... (The Iraqi leaders) were forced to temper their hitherto rigid revolutionary position. the Baghdad Summit appears to have given (them) a taste for diplomacy, as well as a greater awareness that moderate and pragmatic positions could prove far more effective than revolutionary orthodoxy in influencing Arab attitudes and policies".

19. SPRINGBORG, 1985. The quote is from p. 2.

20. KHAFAJI, 1984.

21. **MEES**, 25-2-1980.

22. NIBLOCK, 1982, esp. pp. 139-146, who covers the actual Iraqi - Gulf relations in some detail and whose analysis is the most lucid and coherent yet - although one may disagree with his dismissal of 'subversion' as a motive in Iraqi foreign policy up to the early 1970s. For relations 1975-onwards, see SAKR, 1982, esp. pp. 153-155.

23. See The 1968 Revolution..., pp. 130-133.

24. NIBLOCK, 1982, p. 144

25. There is indeed sufficient evidence of 'change-oriented activities' up to the early 1970s, though not for anything large-scale. According to diplomatic sources, there was clear evidence of Iraqi Baath support for anti-regime activities in Abu Dhabi even in 1976, though this may have had something to do with the continued presence there, in important government positions, of Iraqi expatriates suspected of anti-Baath feelings. See also **Le Monde**, 3-3-1973.

26. **Al-Siyasa**, 19-4-1978

27. **The Middle East Reporter**, 15-3-1980, p. 15

28. BRAUN, 1981, p. 228

29. **SWB**, ME/6340/A/8, 8-2-1980

30. **NYT**, 18-1-1980

31. See NIBLOCK, 1982, p. 143, and SAKR, 1982, pp. 154-155.

32. See for instance **SWB**, ME/6471/A/6-8.

33. **MEES**, 19-5-1980, p. 6

34. **BO**, 16-5-1980; 4-6-1980; **EN**, 3-6-1980

35. **MEED**, 4-7-1980, p. 23

36. **MEES**, 11-8-1980; and XINHUA dispatch, 6-8-1980. For the full text of the communique see **MEES**, 18-8-1980, pp. 3-4.

37. **MEED**, 29-8-1980, pp. 15-16

38. **MEED**, 15-8-1980, p. 11

39. See **BO**, 28-5-1980 and **AR&MEMO**, 2-6-1980.

40. For example, on 21 October, 1979, Dr. Saadun Hammadi, then Iraqi Minister of Foreign Affairs, said in **Al-Thawra** that Iraq did not agree to the formation of Arab blocs which could create negative attitudes to the question of Arab Unity - this even held true for the Euro-Arab oil dialogue, which Iraq wanted to be between the EEC and **all** Arab oil producers.

41. QUANDT, 1981, p. 3

42. ibid., p. 12

43. ibid., pp. 80-82

44. ibid., p. 83

45. NOBLE, 1983, p. 45

46. See SAFRAN, 1985. pp.   280-281; also PISCATORI, 1983, p. 43.

47. See SAFRAN, 1985, pp.   353-354; and QUANDT, 1981, pp. 36-40.

48. QUANDT, 1981, p. 109

49. See SAKR, 1982

50. SAFRAN, 1985: 266

51. See ibid., pp. 266-268

52. **AR&MEMO**, 11-2-1980

53. See also **FT**, 5-2-1980.

54. **NYT**, 18-1-1980

55. **MEED**, 29-2-1980, p. 28

56. SAFRAN, 1985, p. 361

57. **MEES**, 25-2-1980

58. **MEM**, 1981, no. 5
In the UAE there were even rumours that apart from
Pakistan also Iran might be asked to help train the armed
forces (**MEED**, 15-2-1980).

59. **Al-Ra'y al-'Amm**, 15-3-1980

60. **Al-Siyasa**, 27-5-1980

61. **SWB**, ME, 28-5-1980

62. BO, 28-5-1980, and **Al-Khalij**, 31-5-1980

63. **AR&MEMO**, 2-6-1980

64. **MEED**, 2-5-1980, p. 20

65. SWB, ME/6515/a/2,   5-9-1980

66. AT, 8-5-1980

67. EN, 3-6-1980

68. GNA dispatch 20-9-1980

69. MEES, 18-8-1980

70. JANSEN, 1984, p. 82

71. PETERSON, 1983, pp. 160-161. He comments that the
Gulf States would not have wanted the conflict, for fear
of creating "additional tensions among the Gulf's Shi'a
populations". In fact, those tensions were there already,
and rising; the attack was meant precisely to reduce the
danger by lessening Iran's direct influence and
Khomeini's appeal.

72. There were reports of Iranians distributing
subversive literature and possessing arms. See SAKR,
1982, p. 151.

73. WRIGHT, 1980, p. 283

74. ibid., pp. 282-283

75. AMOS, 1984: p. 59; see also SAKR, 1982, p. 151.

76. SAFRAN, 1985, p. 361

77. ibid., p. 364. It is not spelled out what they had
exactly supported.

78. See HUSSEIN, 1979, pp. 74-75 : one of Saddam's main
arguments is that when the economies are interlinked, no
"experiment" taking place in one country will be able to
remain isolated to that country.

79. SAKR, 1982

80. Aswaq al-Khalij, 6-6-1980

81. Contracts for Kuwaiti companies are mentioned in ,
i.a., MEED, 1-8-1980; 22-8-1980; 29-8-1980. For the
irrigation contract see MEED, 12-9-1980, p. 36.

82. See SWB, ME/6471/a/6-8, 12-5-1980; and AT, 8-5-1980.

83. **MEED**, 9-11-1980

84. **MEED**, 30-5-1980, p. 24

85. **MEED**, 15-8-1980, p. 13

86. **MEED**, 8-2-1980; 16-5-1980

87.   See for instance **MEED**, 13-6-1980; **MEES**, 7-1-1980; 28-1-1980, Special Supplement; and 26-5-1980, p.1.

———————————

CHAPTER TWO

POLITICAL ATTITUDES AND RELATIONSHIPS AT THE BEGINNING OF THE WAR, TO OCTOBER 1980

This chapter covers the period of the initial Iraqi blitz followed by the slow advances during October (see Appendix II). There is little specific evidence regarding the Iraqi attitude towards the Arab Gulf states; there were only the not specified visit of "an Iraqi envoy" to Oman during the first week of the fighting (1) and one by Minister of State for Foreign Affairs Hamid Alwan to the UAE on October 27, when he delivered a message from Saddam to Shaikh Zayid (2). However, given the alignment at the eve of the war, one must assume that the attitude was one of expectant supplication. In view of the scale of the aid which would be forthcoming from Kuwait and Saudi Arabia (see Chapter VIII A.), the assumption that agreements had been made on the subject before the outbreak of the war, seems confirmed. This brings us to the attitudes of the Gulf states to Iraq and the war, once full-scale hostilities broke out.

As argued in the first chapter, the Gulf states would have wanted a quick Iraqi victory: the Iranian threat was by far the worst of two evils. They may, later, have begun to value the fact that the extended war weakened both regional powers, but the wide-spread view that they therefore actually wanted to see a prolonged war, must be considered erroneous, in view of the obvious risks of collateral war damage and economic drain. None of them, however, could afford to antagonise an Iran that was not yet beaten. Their oil facilities are extremely vulnerable, and militarily they could not hope to be a match for the Iranian forces. There were obvious differences between them in the proportion of their population composed by Shi'ites, in military strength, and in economic dependence on Iran (UAE trade, for instance, was and is largely Iran-oriented — particularly as regards Dubai), but the evolution of their response to the war was strikingly similar. There were no public statements which revealed their response

in the first days of the fighting - except Iraqi claims
of support - but everything indicates that their initial
stance was   one   of   clear and effective support for the
Iraqi move. This fits in   with   the   context sketched out
above, considering that the Iraqis looked set for a quick
triumph. The Gulf states could justifiably feel there
would be no need for them to become actively involved. To
adopt formally an anti-Iran line was not necessary either
and to do so would   not   have   been   in   keeping with the
careful diplomatic skill they had so far displayed.

The Iraqi News Agency claimed that King Khalid had
personally phoned Saddam to express support in the battle
against "the enemies of the Arab people". The Saudi Press
Agency carried a statement   that   the   King had expressed
"his   interest   and   good   fraternal   feelings",   and
intelligence   reports   indicated   that   the   Kingdom   had
allowed Iraqi warplanes to traverse Saudi airspace and
even to land (3). The official Kuwaiti News Agency
adopted a strongly   pro-Iraqi   tone   (4)   and the country
kept open the land link to Iraq for the transshipment of
goods,   which   became especially vital when Iranian raids
made the northern   tip   of   the   Gulf effectively a no-go
zone. The UAE was something of a special case in that its
press, contrary to that of the other   countries,   added no
comment   to   factual   agency   and   correspondence reports
about events on the front (5).   This   may be explained by
that country's greater vulnerability (6),   its   large
Iranian   community (vital   particularly   to   the   Dubai
economy)(7),   and   the   already   mentioned economic links
with Iran. Zayid is said   to have opposed Khomeini's rise
to power, and the Al-Maktum had enjoyed friendly
relations with the Shah; but the Dubai ruling   family, in
keeping   with   their customary pragmatism, reportedly did
not allow past friendship to   become an obstacle to their
privately   establishing   (together   with   Umm al-Qaiwain)
good relations with the revolutionary regime (8). Sharjah
and to a lesser extent Umm al-Qaiwain since the early
1970s have had a large stake in Iranian cooperation in
the exploitation of the off-shore oilfield around the
Tunbs. A considerable portion of Sharjah's income is
derived from this (9); it could not be expected to place
that income in jeopardy. Reports suggesting that
several emirates would back an Iraqi invasion of Abu Musa
and the Tunbs, would, therefore, seem to have held true
only for Ras al-Khaimah. This ties in with Shaikh Saqr's
stance before the outbreak of the war (see Ch. I),
although he had expressed his hopes   for   a   peaceful
restoration of the islands. Abu Dhabi was reported to
have been prepared to give shelter to Iraqi planes and
ships, but not to cooperate in such a raid (10). It seems

clear therefore, that from the start of the war there was a difference in opinion within the UAE between on the one hand Abu Dhabi, Ras al-Khaimah, and presumably Ajman and Fujairah, and on the other hand Dubai, Sharjah and Umm al-Qaiwain.

Bahrain's regime in the early days of the war "seems to have felt that it could deal with its Shi'ite problem by giving Iraq political support and by allowing Iraqi fighters to disperse in Bahrain"(11). As for Oman, several reports state that Iraq was originally given permission to use bases in the country to reconquer the three islands, a permission only withdrawn after pressure from the West (12). All an Omani official would confirm was that two Iraqi transport planes had landed during the first days of the war (13).

After the first blitz failed to produce the end of the 'limited' war, and Iran began threatening the Gulf states for cooperating with Iraq, they quickly confirmed their official neutral stand. It is plausible that US presure may have had something to do with that (14). Saudi Arabia insisted that the phone call to Saddam had only expressed "concern and brotherly feelings" for Iraq (15). Apparently the planes that had been allowed to land were sent back when the USAWACS arrived and the plans for reconquering the three islands were abandoned (16). The Kuwaiti government denied any active involvement in the war and implored the belligerents to settle the conflict peacefully (17) - a stand which was not contrary to the Iraqi position, as Iraq had accepted, on 28 September, a U.N. cease-fire appeal (18). Bahrain and the UAE insisted they were strictly neutral (19), with Dubai maintaining trade with both sides, accepting distressed cargo for Iraq, but under 'strictly business' conditions (20). Oman also back-tracked, as already indicated, but its position was somewhat enigmatic; Qabus for instance declined to comment on the war in an early October interview (21), and on 7 October convened a meeting of senior military Gulf officers with the reported attendance of a senior Iraqi army officer (22).

The latter meeting is one indication that the Gulf states were effectively on Iraq's side, an impression further strengthened by the tone of most of the region's newspapers (23) - though the stiffening Iranian resistance certainly heightened governmental anxieties. There is no evidence on which to decide whether any of the Gulf states were already giving financial assistance to Iraq at this time (see Ch. VIII, A), but if they were not, that would simply have been because no one at that stage deemed it necessary, considering Iraq's massive reserves and the presumed limited duration of the war.

NOTES TO CHAPTER II

1. **MEED**, 21-11-1980, p. 7, quoting the Omani Undersecretary of Foreign Affairs.

2. WAM dispatch 27-10-1980

3. See **EIU QER, Saudi Arabia**, 1980,4, p.4; and **Time**, 13-10-1980. Confirmed (for "Saudi Arabia and other Gulf states") in HELLER, 1984, pp. 14-15. SPA statement quoted in SAFRAN, 1985, p. 368.

4. **Time** , 13-10-1980

5. Noticed by **The Times**, 24-9-1980

6. A vulnerability study carried out later in Abu Dhabi indiated that an attack on power and desalination plants would mean an immediate crisis. See CORDESMAN, 1984, p. 605.

7. Ibid., notes that "Dubai has upto 100,000 Shi'ites and a strike has proven that its port cannot operate without Iranian workers".

8. Ibid.

9. See ibid., pp. 417 and 419.

10. Ibid. The Iranians accused the UAE and other Gulf states of sheltering Iraqi warplanes and vessels : **MEED**, 3-10-1980. See also SALAMEH, 1984, p. 17, who reports Shaikh Zayid and Saudi Arabia as opposing such close cooperation in the proposed Iraqi raid.

11. CORDESMAN, 1984, p. 588

12. See **Strategy Week**, 20-10-1980, p. 6; CORDESMAN, 1984, p. 397.

13. See note 1.

14. According to HELMS, "Some Arabs have complained privately that their offers of support were constrained by the pressure of the United States, which foresaw a spread of the war if Arab states intervened in a siginificant manner" (1983, p. 81).

15. The King was also said to have prayed to Allah "to grant what is best for our Arab and Muslim world"; see **Time**, 13-10-1980, p. 16, **and EIU QER, Saudi Arabia**, 1980,4, p. 4.

16. See **EIU QER, Saudi Arabia**, 1980,4, p.4.

17. See ibid.; **Time**, 13-10-1980, p. 16; and **MEED**, 10-10-1980, p. 37: wounded soldiers from both sides, they said, were being treated in Kuwaiti hospitals.

18. NONNEMAN, 1984, p. 557

19. **EIU QER Saudi Arabia**, 1980,4, p. 4.; **Time**, 13-10-1980, p. 16; and CORDESMAN, 1984, pp. 588 and 605.

20. See **MEED**, 17-10-1980, p. 17.

21. On 4-10-1980, reported in **MEED**, 10-10-1980, p. 18.

22. The meeting went unreported officially but **MEED** (21-11-1980, p. 7) is confident that its sources for the information are "astute and reliable".

23. WRIGHT even maintains that "Iraqi pride in its (autumn 1980 military) achievement ... is widely shared throughout the Arab Gulf states, where a sense of grievance against Iranian imperialism has been nursed for more than two generations (1980, p. 297).

CHAPTER THREE

POLITICAL ATTITUDES AND RELATIONSHIPS, NOVEMBER 1980 TO
LATE SEPTEMBER 1981

This period is one of stalemate, though to a certain
extent the initiative can still be said to have rested
with Iraq upto late March 1981; that certainly ceased to
be true from April (see App. II). Apart from that, two
facts were of particular importance. First, the loss of
Fao as an oil export terminal due to Iranian air and
naval raids on 29 and 30 November (1) (with the obvious
Iranian intention to strike again when necessary), which
had the long-term effect of drastically lowering revenues
for Iraq. Second, the Iranian air raids on Kuwaiti
territory and installations, on 12 November – bringing
immediate pledges of support for Kuwait from Saudi
Arabia, Bahrain and Qatar (2) – and in December 1980 and
June 1981 (3).

Attitudes of the Arab Gulf states towards Iraq

The air raids on Kuwait catalysed feelings in the Gulf
states against Iran. At the same time it became clear
that the war could become one of attrition, and that Iran
remained very much a military threat. It became therefore
even more of a necessity for the Gulf states to maintain
official neutrality, while in fact stepping up effective
support for Iraq and ensuring that they were not seen to
condone any Iranian behaviour of a threatening nature
towards the Gulf.

The Arab Summit in Amman in November looked, after the
Foreign Ministers of Syria, Libya, Algeria, South Yemen
and the PLO walked out on the eve of the first session,
"dangerously like a Saddam Hussein Supporters' Club" (4),
which as far as Jordan and the Arab Gulf states were
concerned it in fact was. The six Gulf rulers met with
Saddam before the Summit (5). The Conference in its
official communique called for an immediate cease-fire
and a peaceful settlement of the dispute. This was wholly
in agreement with what Iraq wanted at this stage: the

communique praised Iraq for responding positively to the
different international calls for a cease-fire. Moreover
the Conference supported "Iraq's legitimate rights over
its territory and its waters in accordance with the
international agreements signed by the two countries"
(6). Still, it was by no means an anti-Iranian manifesto.

Support for Iraq, however, did not mean that all the
traditional wariness on the Gulf states' part of too
close a relationship with Iraq had been dissipated. When
working out proposals for collective security
arrangements and eventually more wide-ranging integration
- which seemed vital in the increasingly dangerous
environment the Gulf presented, particularly for Saudi
Arabia after the events in Mecca - Iraq was never
considered as a possible partner (although they did
apparently inform Saddam of their plans at the Amman
Summit in November). It had begun to look as if the
Iranian regime would continue to present a threat for the
forseeable future, such that Iraq might be rather more of
a liability than an asset. As indicated before, Iraq had
also always opposed the formation of such a regional
bloc, and in any looser, ideologically acceptable,
regional arrangement would have insisted on being
included, preferrably in a preeminent position. The way
the war was going, therefore, not only made it more
necessary for the Arab Gulf states to come together, but
also, by tying Iraq up, made it possible for them to do
so. A framework for close political cooperation for the
six politically similar conservative monarchies was set
up with the establishment in May 1981 of the
Cooperation Council for the States of the Arab Gulf (or
Gulf Cooperation Council - GCC) (7). The Six (as they
will be referred to henceforth) did all they could to
dispel the impression that the Council actively excluded
Iraq for political or security reasons, or that it
constituted a Western-allied military pact. They stressed
the aim was cooperation, not against anyone but among
themselves , in the spirit of Arab Unity and within the
framework of the Arab League Charter. They underlined the
similarity of their economies, societies and political
systems (8), which of course implied that Iraq could not
fruitfully be included, although that was not as yet made
explicit (9).

Heightened Saudi concern over the direction events were
taking, and the Kingdom's continued support for Iraq, are
indicated by the increased number in Saudi-initiated
diplomatic contacts with the Iraqis in this period,
particularly in the second phase since April (see App.
III). Following the meeting of Prince Abdullah Ibn

Abdul-Aziz with Saddam on 25 September 1981, it was announced that "Iraqi and Saudi viewpoints on matters discussed were identical"(10). At the beginning of the period , after the Iranian attacks on Kuwait, the Saudis reportedly requested Iraq to recall the aircraft it had sent there for shelter (11), presumably anxious not to be seen as an Iraqi forward base. But as time went on, other considerations clearly became more important. Saudi financial aid to Iraq began to flow in 1981 and amounted to at least $ 6 billion over this period. The Saudis also helped Iraq keep its share of the oil market by selling "war relief crude" to affected buyers of Iraqi oil (for this and other aid, see Ch. VIII, A). Saudi Red Sea ports became important transit points for Iraqi imports. From November 1980 there were reports of arms and ammunition supplies, mainly East European and Soviet, going that way, and steadily rising during 1981 such that by the end of the period under consideration more arms were reported to be reaching Iraq via Saudi Arabia than by any other route (12). In September, Shaikh Yamani disclosed that the Iraqis had been given an agreement on principle (though not on specifics) to building a crude oil pipeline across the Kingdom to the Red Sea (13). Saudi Arabia thus firmly took the Iraqi side, breaking off relations with Libya partly over the issue of this alliance (14), but keeping up a careful diplomatic 'neutral' front. The Saudi government also remained effectively neutral in the Syrian-Iraqi rivalry: it did not wish to lose its influence in the Levant.

Kuwait, though protesting against the Iranian attacks, now could not but face the reality of its extreme vulnerability and the necessity of officially adopting a neutral position. When Iran claimed that arms for Iraq had passed through Kuwaiti ports, the country therefore vehemently denied this (15). Effectively however, with Kuwait providing substantial financial aid (Ch. VIII, A) and continued transshipment facilities to Iraq, there was no room for doubt whose side the Emirate was on. Nevertheless, it kept denying Iraq use of Warba and Bubiyan and was, precisely because of its vital support, in a strong enough position to refuse the Iraqi offer of a favourable border settlement in exchange (16).

Oman, which had supported Iraq rather too overtly in the first ʿphase of the war, faced Iranian threats of military action and in late 1980 almost clashed with the Iranian navy in a naval incident. This led Qabus to work out a modus vivendi with Iran, to the effect that he would not take Iraq's side militarily nor interfere with Iranian patrol flights, and Iran would refrain from

sending ships into Omani waters (17). This put a damper
on the previously growing Iraqi-Omani relations (Qabus
had met with Saddam at the Amman summit, and rumours
abounded of a proposed Iraqi-Omani regional security
project (18)). Though remaining politically part of the
pro-Iraqi camp, Oman henceforth would put only very
limited weight on the scales.

The others, too, all called for a peaceful solution and
maintained a neutral front. For Bahrain there was not
much else it could do, since it had neither economic nor
military strength and harboured a considerable number of
supporters of Iran among its Shi'a population. But the
government dealt firmly with pro-Iranian demonstrations
(19). Qatar and the UAE maintained a low-key approach,
but both provided Iraq with considerable financial
assistance (Ch. VIII, A). Attitudes within the UAE
continued to diverge.

Iraq's attitude towards the Gulf states

Because of the changing nature of the war, Iraq was
becoming progressively more dependent upon support from
others, and especially the Gulf states. This inevitably
had an impact on Iraqi attitudes. The Iraqi government
sent out high-level messengers to its main 'providers'
(see App. III), albeit not to Qatar (presumably because
there was no need to, because of Saudi-Qatari
coordination). Iraqi reaction to the formation of the GCC
was not immediately clear. Initially, Foreign Minister
Saadun Hammadi was non-committal, saying that Iraq
welcomed any form of cooperation among Arab countries,
but that it was "too early to say whether the GCC would
take the form of a pact or just a cooperation council
which Iraq could support". Apparently not wanting, as yet,
to put the blame on the Gulf states for excluding Iraq,
he indicated that Iraq had remained outside it because of
its stated policy of not joining cooperation groupings
within the Arab world - favouring instead cooperation
within the framework of the Arab League (20). But when
the new Council had become a fact, Saddam in a 4 July
interview with the Kuwaiti **Al-Anbaa'** stated bitterly that
it was "inconceivable for the Gulf powers to meet and
leave Iraq out at a time when the Iraqi forces are
fighting for the sake of Iraq and yourselves at the same
time". He disclosed that he had already spoken about this
matter to Fahd at the Amman Summit and had told him that
Iraq should not be left out. Although he called the
setting up of the GCC "embarrassing" for Iraq and painful

to him personally, however, he seemed to keep his options open when adding that "despite this, (he) hope(d) that every combined action in the Gulf (would) develop soon so as to protect the whole region against foreigners" (21).

The matter introduced a temporary degree of bitterness in Iraqi-Gulf relations, especially in relations with Saudi Arabia. Since no further declarations of a similar tone were forthcoming, however, one may assume that the Saudi official visits (three out of the four took place after the publication of the interview) and effective aid managed to smooth things over and to make Saddam realise he was not really in a position to be too critical. Indeed, WRIGHT cites an incident in August and September 1981 when, after sharply though not explicitly criticizing Saudi Arabia on its oil policy, the Iraqis almost literally swallowed their words, putting the blame on a journalist (22). Irritation with the UAE (in the same interview Saddam criticised Zayid for not coming out actively enough in support of Iraq after the Israeli raid on the Tammuz reactor) may have been the result of that country's ambivalent attitude and of the fact that the aid given was less than expected (Ch. VIII, A).

Iraqi diplomatic activity in the Gulf was focussed on Kuwait in this period, aimed at convincing the Kuwaitis not to give in to Iranian threats, and at obtaining from them a 99-year lease on Bubiyan: it was now more important than ever to gain a stronger strategic foothold beside its own Gulf-coast. The Iraqis tried to goad Kuwait into accepting by offering them a final border settlement in return - a tack they were also employing with Jordan and Turkey at the time. Such hopes as they entertained for the February 1981 border talks - held at Iraq's request - were however soon dashed by Kuwait's unwillingness to consider any such arrangement (23). Realising its need for Kuwait's continued cooperation, Iraq opted for an approach of honey and acid. On the one hand, after the bomb blasts of late June in Kuwait, Saddam warned Palestinians and others living in Iraq not to jeopardise Iraq's relations with Arab states and particularly Kuwait with whom "close, brotherly relations" existed (24). He stated that Iraq was prepared to arrest and extradite the two Palestinians involved in the blasts who had fled to Iraq, "if this was in Kuwait's interests" (25). But at the same time he publicly reiterated, in an interview with a Kuwaiti newspaper, Iraq's demand for a 99-year lease on part of Bubiyan. Iraq, he said, wanted to build a naval base there "for the defence of Iraq and Kuwait", unless another part of

Kuwait could be made available. He added pointedly: "the settlement of the border problem is entirely in the hands of our Kuwaiti brothers. It needs a decision from you" (26). But there was no official reaction. In an attempt to reduce Kuwaiti concern, Tariq Aziz later that month denied that Iraq wanted a leadership role in the area while confirming that "Kuwaiti security is considered as part of our own" (27).

There were, as in the first period, no recorded high-level diplomatic exchanges between Iraq and Bahrain, Qatar or Oman, except for Saddam's meeting with the rulers during the Amman Summit. As already pointed out, that meeting had particular importance for Iraqi-Omani relations. That the Omanis later changed their stance under Iranian pressure, did not directly affect Iraq's positive attitude: in mid-March 1981, Iraq withdrew its recognition of the Popular Front for the Liberation of Oman (PFLO) and the PFLO-representatives in Baghdad were expelled (28). This, however, was a gesture as much towards the other Gulf states as towards Oman.

Conclusion

Iraq's growing dependence on the Gulf states was reflected in its attitude. While still powerful in the beginning of this period, ideology gradually diminished in importance as a cause for unsettlement in Iraq's relations with the Six. The strategic factor, however, remained a point of friction with Kuwait.

For the Gulf states the whole pre-war configuration upon which they had based their policies, had changed. Positively, the initial aim of weakening Iran and Khomeini's appeal to the local population had been achieved (29). There was therefore no longer any pressing need for the war. Negatively, the Gulf states had never contemplated a drawn-out conflict, which the war was now becoming, with its implications of economic drain and eventually the military threat. The need to avoid these dangers was more important than anything which could be gained from further bleeding the two combatants. Thus the main concern for the Gulf states became to bring the war to an end. This was identical to Iraq's wishes. Officially taking a neutral line, the Gulf states thus remained objectively on Iraq's side. The second imperative was now to prevent an Iranian victory; vital

support   was   provided, with the Saudi government leading
the way.

———————

NOTES TO CHAPTER III

1. STAUDENMAIER, 1983, p. 4

2. **MEES**, 17-11-1980, p. 8. On 26-11 Rafsanjani described the attack on Abdali as a mistake (**FT**, 27-11-1980).

3. **KEESING'S**, 1982, p. 31523. Kuwait accused Iran openly, but responsibility for the raid was denied by Iran.

4. **MEED**, 28-11-1980, p. 15

5. **MEES**, 1-12-1980

6. **MEES**, 8-12-1980

7. This is not the place to elaborate on the creation of the GCC. In late Nov. 1980 the Saudi government said that proposals for a collective security pact had been sent to the five other Gulf states (**MEES**, 1-12-1980). These proposals are thought to have constituted the basis for the talks between the six Foreign Ministers in Riyadh in February 1981, where a Kuwaiti working paper - making no overt reference to security - included the basic propositions for what was to become the GCC (See **MEED**, 6-2-1981, p. 9; 13-2-1981, p. 8).

8. See **Al-Watan al-'Arabi**, 13-2-1981;   **EN**, 5-7-1981; **Arabia**, 1981, no. 1, p. 29.

9. The Bahraini Foreign Minister merely said, in August 1981, that "up to now Iraq nor any other state has asked to be included in the Council" (**Al-Sharq al-awsat**, 22-7-1980). Early on, some Kuwaiti sources had even indicated that "any other Gulf state" could join (**Al-Watan al-'Arabi**, 13-2-1981, pp. 25-26).

10. **Arab News**, 26-9-1980

11. HELLER, 1984, p. 15

12. **MEED**, 28-11-1980, p. 14. According to the Egyptian weekly **October** some of the Egyptian arms supplies to Iraq were sent via Saudi Arabia: **MEED**, 17-4-1980, p. 4; the autumn 1980 assessment is QUANDT's (1981, p. 21): "Early in 1981 the Saudis allowed Iraq to take delivery of 100 East European tanks at Saudi Red Sea ports. This soon became a regular practice,with East European and Soviet ships calling at the small port of Qadima north of Jidda to unload shipments of arms for Iraq". See also **FT**,

6-2-1981.

13. **MEED**, 25-9-1981, p. 42

14. Qaddhafi urged the Saudis to take the Iranian side and to send back the AWACS. When the Kingdom did not comply, he declared a **jihad** against the "American occupation of the Holy Places" (**MEES**, 3-11-1980).

15. **MEED**, 19-12-1980, p. 55

16. The border talks for which Saadun Shakir came to Kuwait on 10-12-1980 took place at Iraq's request. Shakir had to leave Kuwait, however, without achieving any of the hoped-for results (**Al-Qabas**, 15-1-1981; **Arab Times**, 12-2-1981; WRIGHT, 1983, p. 184).

17. See CORDESMAN, 1984, p. 439.

18. See **Al-Siyasa**, 3-12-1980; **EIU QER, B-Q-O-Y**, 1980,4,p.
19. The project would reportedly have involved setting up a joint Arab naval facility in Khasab (Musandam) with Iraqi vessels patrolling the northern and Saudi vessels the middle stretches of the Gulf. This may have been an outcome of the military discussions in Oman (see Chapter II).

19. See **MEED**, 12-12-1980, p. 3.

20. At a press conference in London: see **MEES**, 16-3-1981, p. 7.

21. See his interview with **Al-Anbaa'** on 4-7-1981.

22. See WRIGHT, 1983, p. 182.

23. See **Al-Qabas**, 15-1-1981; **MEED**, 23-1-1981, p. 20; 28-8-1981, p. 20; **Arab Times**, 12-2-1981.

24. AFP dispatch 30-6-1980

25. **Al-Anbaa'**, 4-7-1980

26. Ibid.

27. **Al-Siyasa**, 23-7-1981

28. REUTER dispatch 16-3-1981

29. As does DAWISHA, 1981b , p. 59.

———————

CHAPTER FOUR

POLITICAL ATTITUDES AND RELATIONSHIPS, 28 SEPTEMBER, 1981
TO JUNE 1982

From 28 September 1981, when the Iranians broke the
siege of Abadan, they began recovering ground. This
turned into a counter-offensive proper from 22 March,
1982, a second phase in which the situation for Iraq
became even more serious by the Syrian decision to close
the pipeline carrying Iraqi crude to Tripoli (see App.
II). Other important events characterizing this period
were the Israeli annexation of the Golan - causing a
temporary upsurge in Pan-Arab feeling - and the coup
attempt in Bahrain in December 1981, which reinforced the
Gulf regimes' anti-Iranian feelings. Also, in recognition
of Iraq's changed attitude to international politics, the
country was taken off the US list of countries supporting
terrorism, on 26 February, 1982.

The renewed sense of Arab solidarity after the Israeli
annexation of the Golan led Syria to end its rift with
Saudi Arabia, declaring that it would no longer suppport
Iran if it invaded Iraq, and to help Kuwait in seeking a
peaceful settlement to the war. The peace moves were
backed by Algeria and the PLO, and even Libya agreed to
restore diplomatic relations with Saudi Arabia and Iraq.
There were, furthermore, moves to reconvene the Fez
summit, which had failed in November 1981, when Iraq
(together with the rejection front) had voted against
Fahd's peace plan (1). For a time, therefore, it looked
as if the Gulf states' balancing act was going to be
made easier, thanks to the emerging consensus. This was
indeed very welcome in the increasingly threatening
context of the war. The solidarity would not last, but
Iraq had sensed the possibilities of using it to bring
about an end to the war. This, combined with the even
greater military threat facing Iraq since April 1982 and
its need for Saudi support, eventually led Iraq to
reconsider its stand on the Fahd Plan.

The GCC, meanwhile, had consolidated itself as a distinct
entity, from which new members were now explicitly

excluded (2). Iraq soft-stepped the issue, with Taha
Yassin Ramadhan saying in late October 1981 that
membership "appeared to include other conditions than
geographical location". He added that he hoped the new
body would not prove a new obstacle to Arab Unity (3).
Collectively, the GCC did not take an anti-Iranian
posture. Although after the closure of the Syrian
pipeline it was reported that the Six were discussing
increased aid to Iraq (4), this probably meant that the
Saudi government was advising this. The only substantial
increase in aid, in any case, came from Saudi Arabia and
Kuwait (see Ch. VIII, A). On 30 May, after the Iranians
had recaptured Khorramshahr and looked poised to continue
their march, Iraq called on the Arab states to provide it
with unqualified support and break off relations with
Iran (5). The Six were equally alarmed at the evolution
of the fighting and on the same day their Foreign
Ministers gathered in Riyadh. Iran, however, issued
threats of its own, implying that only a change of
attitude could save the Gulf states from Iranian and
Islamic revenge. As usual, therefore, the fears of the
five smaller members found expression in the communique
issued after the Foreign Ministers' meeting, such that a
neutral tone was maintained - appealing to Iran to
respond to peace initiatives, and supporting the efforts
of the UN, the Non-Aligned Movement, and the Islamic
Conference Organisation (ICO). Particular attention was
drawn to the ICO's mediation committee, which was meeting
in Jeddah a few days later. This, and the extensive
consultations in which the Six were involved with other
Arab capitals, lent plausibility to speculations that the
Six in early July 1982 suggested secret proposals to Iraq
and Iran which would have included the Six paying war
reparations to Iran and helping Iraq with reconstruction
costs (6).

As hinted above and as had already become clear in the
previous period, Saudi Arabia took the most clearly
pro-Iraqi line. During the period treated here, this was
manifest not only in the effective help provided, but
increasingly also in an overtly pro-Iraqi stand, critical
of Iran. The deteriorating Iraqi position on the
battlefield was one element responsible for this
strengthened stand, but two other factors more
specifically influenced the Saudi attitude. The first was
the clashes, in Mecca in October 1981, between Iranian
pilgrims who had staged a demonstration with such slogans
as "Revolution ! Khomeini is the leader", and Saudi
security forces. King Khalid had protested to Khomeini
but the Iranian leader responded that "the ban on
pilgrims interfering in politics is in the interests of

America, Israel and other enemies of Islam" (7). In the
atmosphere of growing irritation with Iranian behaviour,
the newspaper **Okaz** was allowed to accuse Khomeini of
cooperating with Israel in diverting Iraq's energy (8).
The second factor was the coup-attempt in Bahrain in
December. On the 17th of that month the Bahraini
government announced that with the help of Saudi Arabia
65 plotters had been arrested. The Bahraini Minister of
Interior was quite specific in his accusation: "the
saboteurs were sent from Iran" and "(the) sabotage
network (was) being financed by Iran" (9). Without delay,
a security agreement with Saudi Arabia was signed, and
though Bahrain itself appears to have reverted to a more
low key approach, the Saudis attacked Iran in the
harshest terms. After the signing of the security
agreement in Manama, Interior Minister Prince Nayif not
only directly accused Iran as being responsible for the
plot, but said that the country had become "the terrorist
of the Gulf" (10). He stated the Saudi position on the
war as follows:

> As is known, the Gulf countries and many Arab
> countries support Iraq in view of the fact that it
> is an Arab country, a member of the Arab League
> and a signatory to the joint defence charter.
> However, this does not mean that these countries
> want war between Iraq and Iran. They want the war
> to end. (...) It should be known that as Arabs we
> cannot remain neutral and leave Iraq alone in the
> arena. It was Iran that transgressed, and Iraq has
> acted to defend itself. Therefore, our stand must
> be an Arab stand in support of Iraq; at the same
> time, we must work to bring about an end to the
> war (11).

A few days later, on 26 December, Nayif went to Baghdad
to sign a definitive border agreement (basically the
never ratified 1975 agreement) and to spend several days
discussing Gulf security. He stated on that occasion that
Iraq was at war with Iran "not in defence of its lands
and sovereignty alone, but also of the whole Arab
Nation". Saudi support for Iraq, which example Nayif
urged the other Arab states to follow, was dictated by
"religious faith and national duty" (12). Shortly
afterwards a Saudi newspaper even supported Iraq's
request that the Arab states should sever diplomatic
relations with Iran (13). These developments may well
have encouraged Iraq's change of heart on the Fahd Plan
and a further shift in its foreign policy orientation.
Significantly, Taha Yassin Ramadhan went to Riyadh in
early February, with a message from Saddam to King Khalid

and for talks with Fahd and Saud al-Faysal, precisely
when US Secretary of Defence Weinberger was visiting the
Kingdom (14).

When the situation for Iraq worsened further in March and
April, Prince Sultan was dispatched to Baghdad with
messages of support, and a Saudi newspaper quoted Prince
Nayif again as calling Iran the "terrorist of the Gulf"
and as describing the war as part of a conflict between
Iran and all the Arab Gulf states (15). Direct financial
assistance to Iraq during 1982 seems to have been
replaced by the adapted "war relief crude" system whereby
the difference between the Saudi and the Iraqi price was
handed over to the Iraqis (Ch. VIII, A).

According to the Iraqi News Agency, the Emirs of Bahrain,
Qatar and Kuwait also sent messages of support to Iraq in
April 1982 (16) - although, as pointed out, that did not
materialise in the overt and full support that
Iraq wanted. Shaikh Zayid sent his Minister of State
for Foreign Affairs to Baghdad with a message for Saddam,
about "bilateral cooperation" (17), but this does not
appear to have led to any immediate effective help. Oman,
Bahrain, and Qatar, as in the previous period, did not
send or receive any high-level delegations to/from
Iraq.

Kuwait, however, had given Iraq another $ 2 billion loan
in December (see Ch. VIII, A), and kept maintaining
Iraq's import lifeline. On 4 October 1981, the Kuwaiti
government announced a decision to recall its ambassador
from Tehran after Iranian air attacks on Kuwaiti oil
installations on 1 October (18). Also significant were
Kuwait's attitudes to Iran's ally, Syria: in February
1982, a government bill requesting $ 48 million for
Kuwait's share in financing the "Arab Deterrent Force"
(largely Syrian) in Lebanon, was rejected by the National
Assembly because of Syria's actions in Lebanon, the
treatment of the Muslim Brotherhood within Syria, and
Syria's support for Iran (19). With the ex-officio votes
of the cabinet members, the National Assembly vote was
reversed, as would happen again in the debates on the
subsequent budgets, but it remains no less indicative of
the feelings among Kuwaitis. An article in **Al-Qabas** in
early June stated that the Arabs would have no choice
but to take sides, if Iran rejected the new GCC peace
initiative (20). The government, however, worked very
hard at keeping up a front of official neutrality, Shaikh
Saad al-Abdallah warning the other Gulf states against
being drawn into the conflict (21), and sought an active
mediating role. The Kuwaiti government approved the

request which emanated from both Iran and Iraq, that
Kuwait should be one of the sites for family visits to
prisoners of war (22). Iraq meanwhile played down the
border question as a "small difference" (23) and pleaded
for financial help, which it obtained. Though exhorting
Gulf states to stand by it, the Iraqi leadership was not
too openly critical of their careful stance.
Interestingly, plans for an Iraqi oil outlet through
Kuwait to the Gulf, announced in 1981, had been dropped
by mid-July 1982 without further explanation (24).

NOTES TO CHAPTER   IV

1. See **MEED**, 1-1-1982, p. 2.

2. Interview of GCC Secretary-General Dr. Bishara with the Saudi **Al-Madina**, 27-3-1982.

3. AFP dispatch 26-10-1981

4. **Al-Ra'y al-'Amm**, 18-4-1982

5. **MEES**, 7-6-1982, p. 12

6. See for instance **MEES**, 7-6-1982, p. 13 (quoting reports to the effect   that $ 25 billion would have been put up); and HEARD-BEY, 1983, pp. 187-188. Some Gulf officials denied the rumours.

7. **KEESING'S**, 1982, p. 31523

8. **Okaz**, 1-12-1981

9. **SWB**, ME/6912/A/8-9, 22-12-1981; **NYT**, 17-12-1981

10. **KEESING'S**, 1982, p. 31523; and REUTER dispatch 26-12-1981

11. **SWB**, ME/6911/i, 22-12-1981

12. AFP dispatches 26 and 27-12-1981; **KEESING'S**, 1982, p. 31523

13. **Al-Jazira**, 4-1-1982; reported in a KUNA dispatch of 5-1-1982

14. KUNA dispatch 9-2-1982

15. **MEED**, 9-4-1982, pp. 3, 19

16. Ibid., p.3

17. REUTER dispatch 7-4-1982

18. **MEJ**, 36, 1982, p.76

19. **MEED**, 26-2-1982, p. 16. They even called for the suspension of al aid to Syria.

20. **Al-Qabas**, 1-6-1982

21. **EN**, 11-2-1982

22. **MEED**, 26-2-1982, p. 36

23. Interview of Hamid Alwan, Minister of State for Foreign Affairs, with **Al-Siyasa**, 22-12-1981.

24. **MEES**, 12-7-1982 (where the announcement of the plan is wrongly dated earlier in 1982).

CHAPTER FIVE

POLITICAL ATTITUDES AND RELATIONSHIPS, 12 JULY 1982 TO FEBRUARY 1984

From 12 July 1982 onwards, Iran carried the war into Iraq in a series of major offensives. At the same time, however, Iraqi morale and organisation improved and, together with renewed Soviet arms supplies and other international support, gradually led to a still Iranian-dominated stalemate. In 1983 Iraq's long-term perspectives improved with the expansion of the capacity of the Turkish pipeline and the prospect of gaining outlets for its oil through Saudi Arabia. But in the mean time the financial situation worsened as a result of the decreasing capacity of the Gulf states to provide direct financial aid : Saudi Arabia's current account deficit for 1983 was some $ 15.5 bn at least (see Appendix V, Table 4)(1).

Iraq from the onset of this period was highly conscious of the extent of its dependence on third parties – both for providing aid and for creating an environment conducive to the attainment of peace. Hence the further cementing of the alliance with Saudi Arabia; hence, also, the preparations to internationalise the conflict (App. II). In order to be able to profit from its rising export capacity, Iraq tried to gain support among the other Gulf states for a rise in its OPEC quota. Apart from the Kingdom and Kuwait, the other Gulf states retreated into a fear-induced actual neutrality, though the UAE's position is unclear. This divergence inhibited full support for Iraq by the GCC in their Summit communiques, though Iran was reprimanded for having crossed the border and for not responding positively to Iraqi and international peace moves (2). Both Saudi Arabia and Kuwait after the Doha 1983 Summit publicly admitted, however, that the GCC had considered the possibility of "direct hostilities with Iran in the event of any closure of the Gulf's shipping lanes by Iran" (3). In that respect, Iraq's internationalisation strategy – by ordering the Super-Etendards, i.a. – was already working.

Relations with Saudi Arabia

Relations between Iraq and Saudi Arabia stood out in that, as was becoming clear in the previous period, they constituted a real alliance - rather than one of subdued friction and fearful support, as in Kuwait's case, or of neutrality as in the case of the other Gulf states. Some evidence of this can be found in the intensification of high-level visits between Iraq and Saudi Arabia (see App. III): thirteen in all, 7 from Iraq (including one visit by Saddam to King Fahd on 15 January 1983), and 6 from Saudi Arabia, all but one of which were by Crown Prince Abdullah. In only 2 out of those 13 cases (the visit of Iraqi Vice-President Taha Muhieddin Maaruf in early December 1982, and that by the Foreign Ministry Undersecretary in late February 1983) was the emissary not received by the respective head of state. This is proportionately far higher than the number of exchanges with any of the other Gulf states in any of the previous periods, and far higher, too, than the rate of Iraqi-Saudi exchanges in the previous periods. It reflects concern for the precarious situation in which Iraq found itself, and the Kingdom's willingness to reassure Iraq and respond to its requests for support. In addition to the visits, King Fahd telephoned Saddam on at least two occasions to express support (4). The Iraqis, from their side, ratified the necessary laws to implement the border agreements without a hitch (5) and, more significantly, approved the face-lifted Fahd-Plan at the resumed Fez-Conference, 9 September 1982 (6).

The Saudis still insisted on a peaceful settlement, calling on both combatants to enter into a dialogue, but were overtly critical of Iran when, in early November 1982, it dismissed out of hand the latest ICO proposals. These proposals included the establishment of an Islamic (i.e. mainly Arab Gulf) fund to cover war reparations, (which confirmed earlier speculations - Ch. IV), and were widely considered to be the best deal the Iranians could expect. At the same time, incidents involving the Saudi police and demonstrating Iranian pilgrims were reported. Saudi feelings were as usual indicated by the tone of newspaper articles, one of them reporting Algerian plans to revive mediation efforts and commenting that if this last effort was rejected too, the Arabs would impose a political and economic boycott on Iran (7). In this initial period it was Iraq that sent emissaries to Riyadh. From January 1983 the Saudis became equally active. In less than a week, Crown Prince Abdullah went to Baghdad three times, the second time

travelling back to Riyadh with Saddam Hussein and
accompanying him back to Baghdad before flying on to
Syria (App. III). Reportedly Saddam, during his visit,
asked for a further $ 7 billion from Saudi Arabia,
Qatar, and the UAE (8). He also obtained the final
confirmation of Saudi agreement on the principle of
building a pipeline through Saudi territory (9)(Ch.
VIII), which constituted on Saudi Arabia's part an act of
political defiance towards Iran. From early 1983, the
Kingdom also started giving 200,000 barrels a day (b/d)
of crude for sale to Iraqi customers (Ch. VIII, A).

This further strengthening of the alliance was reflected
in renewed media attacks on Iran. One February 1983
editorial in **Al-Jazira**, extensively quoted by Riyadh
Radio in its press review, commented:

> The war lost its objective causes and
> justification when Iraq decided to withdraw ... to
> the international border, and when Iraq declared its
> readiness to negotiate with Iran to resolve border
> disputes ... The Iranian regime ... used such
> disputes as a pretext to justify its aggression ...
> and its persistence in continuing the war ... Iran
> had no qualms in seeking assistance from Israel ...
> Such persistence casts doubts on the nature of the
> authorities that are ruling Iran ... The size of the
> losses in lives indictates that the purpose ... is
> not to achieve a military victory in Iraq so much
> as to destroy both Iran's and Iraq's economies. This
> proves that the source of power in Iran is outside
> Iran, a foreign quarter that is hostile to both
> Islamic Iran and Arab Iraq ... (10)

In an interview with **Al-Siyasa** the next month, Crown
Prince Abdullah said that Iran could not "afford to end
the war without risking a disintegration of the internal
front", whereas Saddam enjoyed "firm popular backing"
(11).

This consistent and overt pro-Iraqi stance, in addition
to the the danger of a long-term drain on the Saudi
Treasury due to the war, lend credibility to the reports
that the Saudis helped convince France to deliver the
Super-Etendards to Iraq, not least by paying for the
arrangement (12). Presumably, the aim was to increase
pressure on Iran to accept peace proposals. In fact, the
pipeline project can be seen in the same light. It is
reasonable to assume that in return the Saudis made
Saddam promise not to destroy Kharg or prevent Iranian
oil transports altogether, as they had to take into

account the Iranian threats of retaliation. The strategy
agreed upon by Iraq and Saudi Arabia appears to have been
to build up the pressure while finding out how far the
Iranians could be pushed without inviting an asault on
Arab Gulf oil installations or action to inhibit traffic
through the Strait of Hormuz.

The mere threat of the acquisition of the French planes
obviously not being enough to intimidate the Iranians in
any way, Iraq, after their delivery in October 1983,
carried out some raids on Kharg and a few ships in the
northern Gulf. This did not succeed in softening the
Iranian government, however. Instead, it led to mutual
missile attacks on civilian targets and a new Iranian
offensive in the south, where Iraq was temporarily
brought in a militarily precarious situation (App. II).
In this latest phase, the flow of Saudi messages and
visits in connection with the war increased again (App.
III), while the Saudi media very explicitly sympathised
with Iraq (13).

Relations with Kuwait

Needless to say, the Kuwaiti government perceived the
Iranian thrusts into southern Iraq as a direct danger.
On the one hand this fed the government's fears and
therefore strengthened its official neutral stance. On
the other hand, however, material support for Iraq
remained as neccessary as ever, and both official and
popular irritation with Iran grew. After **ashura**
demonstrations in 1982 by Iranian nationals and
sympathisers of Khomeini in Kuwait, which led to
disturbances, the Kuwaiti government directly accused
Iran of being involved (14). But at the same time the
government made clear that it was not going to give in to
Iraq on the matter of the islands. In early September
1982 a preliminary feasibility study contract for the
development of Bubiyan was awarded (15) and in
mid-October the construction of a bridge between the
mainland and Bubiyan was commissioned. The political
content of this move is confirmed by the fact that
neither of the connected points has any population or
installations, nor connecting roads; and by the
exceptional speed of construction, made possible by
opting for a turn-key project (unusual for Kuwait), a
revolutionary design, and the use of Chinese workers. The
bridge was completed within 5 months (16). There were no
further Iraqi requests for a lease on Bubiyan over this
period, which in part reflects Iraq's dependence on
Kuwaiti assistance. Such assistance was indeed

forthcoming, not only in the continuation of the provision of trans-shipment and other services, but in aid. Kuwait was coming under the same financial constraints as the other Gulf states and there is no evidence of financial aid flows to Iraq after 1982, but from early 1983 Kuwait began giving between 50,000 and 100,000 b/d of Neutral Zone crude for sale to Iraqi customers (see Ch. VIII, A).

As in previous periods, it is interesting to note the attitude of the Kuwaiti National Assembly. That attitude was revealed in the call by several deputies on the government, in January 1983, to hold contacts with Iraq to finalise the demarcation of the border (17), and in the Assembly's support (exclusive of the Cabinet) for a proposal to suspend aid to Syria (18).

Relations with the UAE

The UAE was probably the country on which Iran spent most efforts in trying to woo away from Iraq. This was helped by the attitude adopted by the rulers of Dubai, Sharjah and Umm al-Qaiwain, added to growing UAE fears of external (military) or internal (political or economic) Iranian action. In early November 1982, Iran sent its first ambassador to the UAE since the revolution; the UAE did not officially reciprocate, though a Foreign Affairs Ministry official described relations between the two countries as "friendly" (19). The only official 'UAE-attitude' towards the Gulf War one can talk of at this time was the frequently expressed desire for a peaceful settlement. Otherwise the distinction between mainly Abu Dhabi and Dubai remained. In fact, Abu Dhabi and Ras al-Khaimah can be considered the only emirates to have shown any pro-Iraqi bias at all, though even there evidence is scanty. On the GCC Supreme Council it was of course Shaikh Zayid's voice that was heard. Saddam Hussein thus focussed his attention on Abu Dhabi - the only potential aid donor anyway.

In an interview on 5 December, 1983, Saddam criticized "certain Arab Gulf leaders" because "for fear of the Iranian authorities" they "try to buy them off with bribes , with Syrian advisers as intermediaries". He distinguished between these leaders and "those that have behaved correctly towards Iraq" (20). The only state that could have been implied here was the UAE. Whether the criticism was aimed at Abu Dhabi as well as at Dubai and Sharjah, is hard to establish. On the one hand, only Abu Dhabi would have been able to offer any substantial

"bribes"; and CORDESMAN states that during this period it
"started to make quiet payments to Iran in an effort to
buy security" (21). On the other, there are reports that,
after promising Iraq additional financial aid at the Fez
summit in September 1982, the UAE (read Abu Dhabi)
actually paid up (see Ch. VIII, A). Shaikh Zayid was also
involved in contacts with the Iraqis, both actively, as
peace negotiator (22), and on the receiving end, with
visits from General Humaid Shaaban, (Saddam Hussein's
special adviser on military affairs) in August 1983 (23)
and Oil Minister Ahmad Qasim Taqi in February of the next
year (24). Both carried messages from Saddam; the latter
no doubt contained a plea that the UAE consent to a
higher OPEC quota for Iraq (25).

The evidence is inconclusive. The reports about supposed
financial transfers to Iraq or Iran are not confirmed by
other reliable sources. It is indeed doubtful whether Abu
Dhabi could, from 1983 onwards, afford to give away
billions to one, let alone to both parties. Abu Dhabi
did, in any case, remain next to neutral because of its
growing fear for its own security and in part so as to
safeguard the UAE's cohesion. Sympathy, however, remained
with Iraq rather than with Iran.

The others

The other Gulf states basically maintained their previous
attitude, with Bahrain in particular keeping the lowest
possible profile. The Iranian offensive did, however,
prod Oman and Qatar into some action. The Omani
government in October 1982 decided to recall its Charge
d'Affaires from Tehran in protest against Iran's military
thrusts into Iraq, and to donate $ 10 million to Iraq
(26). In September of the following year, the Qatari
Foreign Minister arrived in Baghdad on a surprise visit -
the first recorded high-level visit from Qatar to Iraq
since the start of the war (App. III). He was received by
Tariq Aziz, but no details about the discussions were
disclosed (27). This was preceded by an Iraqi visit to
the Emirate (also the first) by the Iraqi Oil Minister
Ahmad Qasim Taqi, a visit reportedly part of coordination
efforts among Gulf OAPEC members, but which also involved
discussion on bilateral relations (28). It seems probable
that Iraq asked the Qatari government for aid, and
pleaded its case for an increased OPEC quota. In October,
the Qatari Foreign Minister was again in Baghdad,
attending a meeting between Saddam and Shaikh Zayid -
before travelling on with the former to Syria (29), no
doubt to convince Asad to support peace efforts. Qatar

figured again in the Gulf tour of Taha Yassin Ramadan on
22 October, when he brought messages from Saddam to the
Amir, as well as to Sultan Qabus and Shaikh Isa of
Bahrain, "to explain the situation in the Gulf war" (30).
It is difficult to assess the importance of this higher
Qatari profile - active and passive - but it possibly
reflected on the one hand heightened Qatari concern about
direct war damage, and on the other an Iraqi perception
that the Qatari government (itself coming under financial
constraints) was beginning to waver in its inclination to
follow the Saudi lead.

NOTES TO CHAPTER V

1. WHARTON **FOCI** Vol. 4, 9, (July 15, 1985), p. 10, has $ 18.9 bn.

2. The November 1982 Summit communique said on the war: "The Council discussed the developments in the war between Iraq and Iran. While it follows the serious developments represented by Iran crossing its international border with Iraq and the great threat which these developments pose to the safety and security of the Arab Nation and the violation of its sovereignty, and as it believes that these latest developments have taken place at a time when the Arab Nation is striving to consolidate its solidarity and mobilise its forces to confront the escalating Zionist aggression, ... the Council affirms its support for Iraq in its endeavour to put an end to this war by peaceful means ..." (Read by Secretary-General Bishara on Manama Television, quoted by **SWB**, ME/7182/A/1-2, 13-11-1982). The Six, according to **Al-Riyadh** (12-11-1982) would ask Syria and Algeria to intercede with Iran to stop the war.

At the 4th Summit in Doha, November 1983, the Coucil affirmed its full support for UN Security Council Resolution 540 of October 31 calling on Iran and Iraq to cease all military operations in the Gulf area and to refrain from attacking towns, economic installations and ports. The Council "noted with satisfaction" Iraq's agreement to the solution and it called on Iran to "respond positively" (KEESING'S, 1984, pp. 32648-9).

3. AMIN, 1984, p. 74

4. On 1-10-1982 (**SWB**, ME, 4-10-1982); and on 25-2-1984 (AFP dispatch, 26-2-1984, quoting GNA).

5. **MEED**, 6-8-1982, pp. 15-16

6. GULF NEWS, 11-9-1982

7. SWB, ME, 4-10-1982; **MEES**, 8-11-1982; **NYT**, 25-9-1982; 9-10-1982

8. **MEED**, 4-2-1983, pp. 21-24

9. **MEED**, 25-2-1983, p. 17

10. **SWB**, ME/7256/A/3, 12-2-1983

11. Quoted by **EN**, 23-3-1983

12. See AMIN, 1984, p. 74 (although he appears to confuse the planes with the missiles); **MEI**, 13-9-1985, p.11;

13. See e.g. Radio Riyadh's news analysis on 28-2-1984: **SWB**, ME/7581/A/3, 2-3-1984.

14. **MEES**, 8-11-1982

15. **MEED**, 3-9-1982

16. **MEED**, 15-10-1982, p. 25

17. **AT**, 16-1-1983

18. **EN**, 9-11-1983

19. **MEED**, 5-11-1982, p. 68

20. **Al-Watan al-'Arabi**, 12-5-1983

21. CORDESMAN, 1984, p. 419

22. QNA dispatch, 8-10-1983; **SWB**, ME/7461/A/6, 11-10-1983

23. REUTER dispatch 3-8-1983

24. KUNA dispatch 22-2-1984

25. Taqi told the press about Iraq's increased export capacity and his hope that the quota would be raised. The meeting with Zayid was also attended by Dr. al-Otaiba. (KUNA dispatch 22-2-1984).

26. **IHT**, 13-10-1982, and Chap. VII A. (On 16-10, the Charge d'Affaires was reported still to be in Tehran (**SWB**, ME/7159/i, 18-10-1982, quoting QNA). It is not clear whether he was actually withdrawn.

27. KUNA dispatch 10-9-1983

28. SPA dispatch 26-2-1983

29. QNA dispatch 8-10-1983; **SWB**, ME/7461/A/6, 11-10-1983

30. KUNA dispatch 22-10-1983; REUTER dispatch 23-10-1983

CHAPTER SIX

POLITICAL ATTITUDES AND RELATIONSHIPS, SPRING 1984 TO JANUARY 1986

Iraq's fortunes improved in several ways. Its financial prospects became less severe thanks to the expansion of the pipeline to Dortyol, the Saudi and Kuwaiti oil swaps, and the expectation of further pipeline extensions via Saudi Arabia and possibly Jordan. Consequently, the country's credit rating also improved. At the same time, Iraq's internationalisation strategy, by way of attacking Kharg and tankers in the area, increased international concern and efforts to stop the war. In the wake of the Iranian retaliations on tankers carrying Arab oil, in May 1984, the Gulf states finally came out openly against Iran, condemning it for the attacks and sponsoring a UN Security Council resolution to the same effect (1).

The attacks on Kuwaiti and Saudi tankers provided the spark, but Saudi Arabia had already been pressing the other Arab states and in particular the GCC to harden their attitudes. The GCC Council of Foreign Ministers on 10 March 1984 had praised the Iraqis for their co-operation with the Qatari Amir in his mediation efforts (2). In the one-day emergency session on 14 March of Arab League Foreign Ministers in Baghdad (held at the request of Iraq), the Iranian aggression on and occupation of Iraqi territory was condemned and a call was made for an immediate cease-fire. Syria and Libya boycotted the meeting. A seven-man committee was establishhed with a view to following up peace efforts and convincing Iran's main trading partners to stop dealing with Iran. The main aim appeared to be to cut off arms supplies, and Saudi Arabia (with Iraq) was again the prime advocate (3).

The Iranian attacks followed repeated threats to Saudi Arabia and Kuwait. When an Iranian Phantom was shot down by Saudi F-15s over Saudi territorial waters on 5 June 1984, the volume of Iranian vitriol directed at the Gulf regimes still supporting Iraq increased even further. Thus, Kuwaiti officials were reminded that "if they continue their present policies they wil not be able to separate their fate from that of the mercenary Saddam" (4); the Kuwaiti elite was criticised and the elections ridiculed (5); and the Saudi regime was described as despotic, "plundering their people's national wealth on having a good time in the gambling resorts of Europe and America" and cooperating with Israel (6). This had the effect of making the GCC revert to its earlier style: in the communique of the November 1984 Summit and that of the GCC Foreign Ministers in March 1985, Iraq's rights were supported, its positive stance applauded, and peace negotiations called for, but Iran was not specifically condemned: the Iranian leadership was merely called upon to respond to the peace efforts (7).

With all this, the GCC and more specifically Saudi Arabia and Kuwait did not change their basic policy of support for Iraq. Iran in May 1985 suddenly switched to a different approach and tried to foster better relations with each of the Six. Prince Saud al-Faysal was invited to Tehran, a delegation was sent on a tour of the Gulf states, and the message was put across that Tehran opposed terrorism. The Iranian government denied any involvement in the "Islamic Jihad" , and in the 25 May 1985 assassination attempt on the Kuwaiti Amir in particular. The Iranian leaders stressed their desire for friendly relations with each of the Six (8). This change was no doubt welcomed with some sceptical relief by the Gulf states, but it did not lead them to alter their position significantly. The communique issued after the 15th meeting of GCC Foreign Ministers in July 1985 contained much the same as always, except that Iran's detention of the UASC vessel **Muharraq** was strongly condemned as contravening international law (9).

Consequently, when Iraq in August and September 1985 escalated its attacks on Kharg, for the first time badly impairing Iran's export capacity, and apparently not being held back by Saudi Arabia or Kuwait, the Iranian government again turned to threats of blocking the Strait of Hormuz and to harassing Kuwaiti and other ships on suspicion of carrying supplies to Iraq (10).

In the period leading up to the November 1985 GCC Summit, the Iranian leadership also began to claim it perceived some changes in the Gulf states' attitudes to the war - changes, according to Prime Minister Mussavi, which "have naturally taken place in the light of our firm stands" (11). This was probably simply the well-known device of praising a wavering friend or adversary for his positive stand, hoping that such a stand would then indeed materialise. Nonetheless, the statement which followed the 16th meeting of GCC Foreign Ministers in September, did adopt a 'neutralist' tone, although "Iran's continued refusal to respond to the peace efforts" was regretted, and Kuwait's Shaikh Sabah al-Ahmad affirmed afterwards that "any threat or attack against any Gulf state would be considered a threat and an attack against all the GCC states" (12).

Iran's approach appeared to have some success, in that the six GCC leaders, in their Communique of 6 November, adopted a tone which was less critical of Iran than had previously been the case. This could hardly be termed a substantial change, however, since the suggested basis for peace negotiations were two UN Security Council Resolutions which Iran had already rejected. The part of the Communique pertaining to the war, states:

> The GCC Supreme Council discussed the Iraqi-Iranian war in the light of recent developments and in the light of the serious escalation - particularly in the Gulf waters - and discussed the threat this posed to the security and stability of the entire region and freedom of navigation in the Gulf.

> With regard to the situation in the Gulf region, the Supreme Council recalled what was announced at the conclusion of the fourth session held in Doha in November 1983, which stated its adherence to UN Security Council resolutions Nos. 540 of 1983 and 552 of 1984, which expressed the international community's support for freedom of navigation in international waterways and for freedom of passage of merchant ships from and to the ports of the GCC states. The Supreme Council calls on Iran to respect the principles mentioned in these two resolutions.

> The Supreme Council also affirmed what it had declared in its fifth session in Kuwait in November 1984 regarding the Iraqi-Iranian war, especially its emphasis on the need for the readiness of the GCC states to continue their endeavours with the parties concerned to end this destructive war in a manner that safeguards the legitimate rights and interests of the two sides, in order to bring about normal relations among the Gulf states. (13)

The more even-handed wording of the communique brought praise from Iran, and the Iranian government let it be known that it considered this the first implicit criticism of Iraq (14). Foreign Minister Velayati, in a stepped-up campaign aimed at wooing the Gulf states, was friendly and reassuring:

> The Islamic Republic of Iran is genuine in its intentions to have friendly relations with its neighbours ... We welcome the positive steps recently taken by the Persian Gulf southern littoral states and we have shown that we shall always respond positively to friendly gestures by other countries; just as ... we stand up against any hostile action that emanates from any country, (15)

thus combining the carrot and the stick.

A GCC delegation, headed by the Omani Minister of State for Foreign Affairs, Yusif al-Alawi, was established to renew mediation efforts. The delegation visited Baghdad, but never went to Iran - an indication of the realisation that no common ground would be found. During the talks with Saddam Hussein, on the contrary, al-Alawi had "sensed total understanding with regard to the GCC countries' concept of achieving security, peace and safety and to find the appropriate means to end the current war" (16).

Iraq's attitude to the GCC, meanwhile, remained a hybrid of 'humble' acceptance and 'subtle' pressure, best expressed by Saddam in an interview with visiting Kuwaiti journalists in May 1984. After stating that Iraq did not wish to call itself a Gulf state, he qualified:

> Brothers, when the war is over and you want to set up a Gulf intervention force, I say Iraq is Arab and Iraq is situated on the Gulf. But Iraq is not seeking external manifestations and wants only good for its brothers. Any time that you feel Iraq is in the Gulf and that it is worthy of becoming a Gulf brother at any level of cooperation, we shall study this. It is our conviction that the basis for this is pan-Arab interest (17).

Obviously, the statement that Iraq was not considered a Gulf state should not be taken seriously. Indeed, Taha Yassin Ramadhan in a July 1984 interview said exactly the opposite when explaining the "unique type of relationship between us and other brothers in the Gulf" (18). But the wish to reassure the Six was paramount.

This almost meek attitude, contrasting with Iraq's

earlier regional pretentions, fits into the wider
context of the continuing shift in the country's foreign
policy - partly a logical extension of the pre-war
evolution, partly directly influenced by consideration of
wartime needs. In November 1984, Tariq Aziz told a group
of congressmen that the policy of seeking regional
domination by one country or leader in the area was
outdated - the future, rather, lay in cooperation (19).
Iraq's position by the end of the period under
consideration had in fact softened even further, as a
result of the economic and political pressures to which
the country was subjected. This is clear from the
comments made by Oman's al-Alawi after his talks with
Saddam in December 1985 (quoted above), and was spelled
out by Saddam himself in an interview with the Kuwaiti
Al-Qabas on 5 February 1986:

> We particularly appreciate our brothers in Kuwait
> and Saudi Arabia. As for our other brothers, our
> interest in them is measured by their stand towards
> us ... It is enough for us if any Arab mentions us
> in his prayers in silence if he does not want
> anybody except God to hear his prayers. That is
> enough for us if that Arab cannot extend material
> assistance ... Our brothers in the Gulf have
> adopted a good position in general and Kuwait and
> Saudi Arabia in particular adopted very good
> positions.

This leads us to take a closer look at the individual
relationships.

Relations with Saudi Arabia

Iraqi-Saudi political relations did not change
significantly during this period, but Saudi Arabia's
attitude towards Iran and the Gulf War (and thus by
implication towards Iraq) did undergo some shifts.
Throughout, however, support for Iraq was maintained. One
can deduce from the list of recorded high-level visits
that there was no longer the same level of concern on the
part of the Saudi government for Iraq's security (only
five such visits occurred over this two-year period).
Iraq was again the asking party but felt more
confident, at least after the main spring 1984 offensives
(when it had convened the emergency Arab League meeting).
Only 6 Iraqi delegations to Riyadh are recorded up to and
including July 1985 (none between December 1984 and the
July 1985 visit of Tariq Aziz - see App. III). This
reflected realities on the ground. However, from the

onset of the second main phase in this period (with the
escalation of the attacks on Kharg and tankers carrying
Iranian oil), the Iraqis maintained regular contact with
Riyadh, sending 5 delegations between September 1985
and January 1986. This is explained by their anxiety to
(a) maintain Saudi approval of the changed tactics, and
(b) press the Saudi government to extend the oil-swap
deal which was scheduled to end in January 1986 (see Ch.
VIII).

Several commentators have hinted at the existence of
frictions between Iraq and Saudi Arabia over the
expansion of the tanker war. Iraqi strikes on Saudi
ships were often taken as evidence of and reason for such
friction. However, a close look at all the attacks that
have taken place (20) reveals only two cases where there
is no doubt that the Iraqis deliberately struck at ships
with Saudi capital involvement: these were the attack on
the **Safina al-Arab** on 25 April 1984, and that on the
Al-Ahood on 7 May. In both of those cases, the tankers
were carrying Iranian oil and thus fell under the Iraqi
threat. Large Saudi interests were indeed involved
(Faysal bin Fahd in the case of the **Safina al-Arab**,
Ghaith Pharaon in that of the **Al-Ahood**), but this went
no further than shareholdership in the independent oil
trading companies chartering the tankers and which were
wholly managed by non-Saudis (21). The Saudi government
did not react officially, and Shaikh Yamani tried to play
the matter down further by saying that the Iraqi pilots
could not have known which flag the ships were flying
(22). The latter contention is not only unlikely but was
implicitly contradicted by Saddam in his **Al-Watan**
interview (23). At any rate, it is clear that the Iraqis
had to consider all ships loading Iranian oil equally,
and that the two attacks had no implications for the
formal Iraqi-Saudi relationship. The incident does
indicate, however, that private Saudi interests - even
including the King's son - cared little about Iraq's
wishes. The Saudi government advised tankers flying the
Saudi flag to stay away from Kharg (24). This kind of
pressure was what the Iraqi government was seeking, a
message probably put across when Tariq Aziz flew to
Riyadh on an unscheduled visit on 29 April (25).

As mentioned above, the Saudi government strongly
condemned the Iranian retaliatory raids on Saudi and
Kuwaiti shipping. It urged Arab support for Iraq, and a
senior Foreign Ministry official joined the Kuwaiti and
Iraqi Foreign Ministers on a mission (sent by the 7-man
committee) to Japan to dissuade that country from dealing
with Iran on the same level as with Iraq (26). Around

this time, Saddam reportedly hinted that "the Saudis, with US approval, were leaking occasional intelligence (to Iraq) from the five American AWACS in the Gulf"; this, according to the **Sunday Times**, "turned into a steady flow of information after the restoration of US-Iraqi diplomatic relations" (27).

Events in the mean time took a new turn when, on 5 June 1984, two Saudi F-15 aircraft guided by an AWACS shot down an Iranian F-4 near a Saudi island 40 miles east of the Saudi coast. According to US State Department sources, Saudi aircraft had previously pursued the Iranian attackers of a tanker in late May (28). Prior to that, the Saudi airforce had remained remarkably inactive. This inactivity had been explained by the Saudi regime's reluctance to send its airforce out fully armed (arguably a risk for the regime's own security), as well as its fear of the consequences which would follow from committing supposedly inexperienced pilots against redoubtable adversaries, and of escalating the conflict and drawing the Iranian wrath onto Saudi Arabia. Some importance may be attached to those considerations, and the Saudi government certainly preferred to contain the tanker war. But, having projected itself as the main power in the GCC and having built up a massive and expensive military apparatus (at the price of dependence on American assistance), words and inaction in the face of Iranian attacks on Gulf shipping were no longer an acceptable response. The material superiority of the Saudi over the Iranian airforce was, with this one encounter, translated into an effective superiority, boosting the Saudis' confidence.

Often the Saudi government's subsequent 'embarrassment' and surprise at its own success has been highlighted, implying that the leadership would rather placate the Iranians than risk anything similar again. This impression is erroneous, for although Saudi officials afterwards stressed they did not want an escalation of the conflict – an understandably genuine feeling – they also stressed their determination to protect shipping. Jeddah radio reported how the two pilots who "destroyed the target which launched aggression against [Saudi] territorial waters" and the technicians who had guided them, were honoured with a visit by Prince Sultan at the King Abdul Aziz airbase, were awarded the King Abdul Aziz First Class Badge of Honour (Second Class for the technicians), and had a memorial picture taken with the Prince (29). On 20 June US officials announced that the Kingdom had set up an "air defense interception zone", outside the 12-mile territorial waters limit, within

which the Saudi Airforce would engage aircraft
threatening shipping. Aircraft intruding into the 12-mile
zone would be shot down on sight (30). A corridor was
thus created within which shipping could pass safely. The
limits of that protection became clear when further
attacks on tankers occurred; these attacks, however,
nearly always took place east of Qatar. Arab Gulf oil
transports were therefore not seriously impaired.

Over the following five months, three high-level Iraqi
delegations were received at the highest level (see App.
III). Izzat Ibrahim and his delegation, who were on a
Gulf tour and arrived in Saudi Arabia in August, in
addition to these top-level meetings also met with
Prince Sultan, Shaikh Yamani, the Commerce Minister and
the Deputy Foreign Minister (31). The Saudi government
kept pressing for a peaceful settlement, and did not go
out of its way to offend the Iranians, but was clear in
its support for Iraq (e.g. the above mentioned sharing of
AWACS information) and firm in opposing Iranian threats
to Gulf shipping.

A third phase began when Iran switched to a friendly
approach in May 1985, inviting Prince Saud al-Faysal to
Tehran. The invitation was accepted and the visit took
place on 19 May. For obvious reasons, the Saudis were not
going to reject any opening by Iran, which could reduce
tension in the area and improve Saudi security, possibly
even leading on to negotiations. The tone of the media's
comments changed, and Iran was no longer attacked. But
the polite and somewhat hopeful statements of both Saud
al-Faysal and the Iranian leaders could not hide their
still diametrically opposed views on the war and how it
should end. Both sides were prepared to turn over a new
page as far as bilateral relations were concerned
(Foreign Minister Velayati accepted an invitation to
return the visit), but Iran still insisted on the
"punishment of the aggressor" in the war and the exit of
Saddam, whereas the Saudi statements spoke about the
"clearing up of ambiguities", in order to "achieve a
better understanding of the problems that concerned the
Kingdom and Iran", and about the necessity of ending a
war which presented opportunities "for those who lurk in
ambush", (to harm both countries and Islam) (32). Tension
in Saudi-Iranian relations, therefore, lessened, but the
Saudi attitude towards Iraq did not change. One
indication of this is the continuing supply of
'war-relief crude'; another, the completion of the Iraqi
spur to the Saudi East-West pipeline (Ch. VIII).

As indicated, a discernibly different phase started when

the Iraqis began in earnest to attack Kharg in August and
September 1985, inflicting, this time, heavy damage on
the oil terminal (33). The Saudi government, which so far
had apparently restrained Iraq from going that far, now
evidently no longer did so. It could be argued that the
Iraqi government, confident that Saudi Arabia would not
renege now on its promise to let Iraq use the extra
capacity of the East-West line, and realising that the
time of oil swaps might be over anyway, no longer cared
about Saudi pressure. In that case one must assume some
friction between the two. However, the evidence presented
earlier militates against this view; so does the surge in
high-level contacts which started, significantly, with an
unexpected visit by Izzat Ibrahim to King Fahd on 8
September, prior to the escalation (34). This would seem
to strengthen an alternative explanation, viz. that the
Saudi government had decided to back Iraq in raising
pressure on Iran so as to obtain an end to the war. It
is reasonable to assume that the Saudi leadership felt
strong enough militarily to resist Iranian direct
attacks, and that it did not believe Iran to be willing
or capable to block the Strait of Hormuz (an assessment
which was almost certainly correct). Iraq, indeed, never
showed any dissatisfaction with the Saudi stance. In
July 1984 Taha Yasin Ramadhan stated that Iraq felt
"comfortable with the nature of relations with the Gulf
states, particularly Saudi Arabia and Kuwait" (35). The
Iraqi media spent plenty of space and time on reporting
Saudi Arabia's supportive attitude, and in the February
1986 statement quoted earlier Saddam himself stressed
his satisfaction with the position taken by Saudi
Arabia.

Not surprisingly, then, the Kingdom again became subject
to Iranian threats and verbal attacks. Iran did, however,
slowly revert to its earlier policy of trying to build
bridges, eventually leading to the promised visit by the
Foreign Minister to Riyadh on 7 December - but not before
yet another vitriolic attack, less than a week before the
visit, by Ayatollah Montazeri. Montazeri denounced the
"Wahhabi sect" as "founded by mercenaries affiliated to
foreigners", aiming "to create factionalism and division
between the world's Muslims" and "even to ruin the
honoured grave of the Prophet". The Wahhabi leaders were
described as not having "any faith in Islam or in the
Koran". This "misled Wahhabi sect", was party to a
"colonialist conspiracy" and was responsible for the
poisonous anti-Shi'i propaganda in the region (36).

Velayati's visit carried forward the dialogue begun
during Saud al-Faysal's May visit to Tehran, but did not

initiate any new developments. Both sides agreed again on
the principle of expanding bilateral relations, and
reached some understanding regarding matters of Islam.
Although Velayati, in line with earlier Iranian tactics,
described the talks as "satisfactory", Riyadh radio
commented that "the visit to the Kingdom by HE the
Iranian Foreign Minister did not achieve a decisive,
positive result, given the expected Iranian stance", and
Prince Saud was quoted as saying that he "really did not
sense any development in the Iranian stance that would
imply a positive move towards ending the Iraq-Iran war";
in contrast, Iraq was praised for its "stable and clear
stance" and willingness to work for peace (37).

Relations with Kuwait

The relationship with Kuwait was rather more dubious, for
although that state kept supporting Iraq in words,
oil-swaps and transshipment facilities, friction
re-emerged over the border and islands questions.
Kuwait's posture vis-a-vis Iran, like Saudi Arabia's,
grew firmer in the wake of Iranian attacks on Kuwaiti
ships. It is unlikely that any of those attacks, mistakes
apart, were the responsibility of Iraq (38): no ship with
Kuwaiti official shareholding was involved in oil
liftings from Kharg. After the 13 and 14 May attacks on
Kuwaiti ships, Kuwait officially accused and sharply
criticized Iran. It was Kuwait which, on 16 May 1984,
asked for an emergency session of the GCC, leading to the
above-mentioned condemnation of Iran and sponsorhip of
the subsequent UN Security Council resolution (39).

Kuwait, like Saudi Arabia, hoped that tension with Iran
could be reduced, and welcomed the Iranian change of
attitude from May 1985 onwards. Iran was not directly
accused of involvement in the assassination attempt on
the Amir on 25 May (40). As Kuwait's effective support
for Iraq had not diminished, the lull in tension was
unlikely to last. Moreover, the deportation of several
thousand people of Iranian stock (recent arrivals and
others) prompted unfavourable publicity in Iran. Already
towards the end of July a Kuwaiti ship was held by the
Iranians for inspection. Subsequently goods from several
others , supposedly en route for Iraq, have been
confiscated (41). The Kuwaiti Foreign Minister, Shaikh
Sabah al-Ahmad Al-Sabah, was reported in July 1984 to
have stated, that "Kuwait would continue to support Iraq
because there were treaties and charters that could not
be abandoned and because Iraq is an Arab country" (42).
After the visit of Izzat Ibrahim and his delegation in

August 1984 (see App. III) the Kuwaiti press release stated that Iraq had praised Kuwait's continuing support in various fields, and that Shaikh Saad praised "the Iraqi people and army for their heroic defence of the Arab right and their positive response to all peace initiatives in the Gulf War" (43).

After the heavy Iraqi attack on Kharg (15 August 1985), the Kuwaiti daily **al-Siyasa** commented, that Iraq had "carried out an operation which it had been contemplating for a long time and had timed perfectly. Iran is very much mistaken if it contemplates retaliation. The states overlooking the Gulf are now capable of double retaliation". Commenting on the situation in Iran, the paper added that "the rational people there are not in control or in a responsible position" (44). Iran responded via its media. The Iranian News Agency carried a lengthy quote from an editorial in the paper **Ettela'at**, in which Kuwait was accused of hostile actions, including collaboration with Iraq in attacking Iran's oil installations, torture and expulsion of Iranians, and obstructing the Afghan Mujahidin's struggle by entering into secret dealings with the Soviets. For the paper, Kuwait's actions could legitimately be interpreted as a declaration of war, and they should thus be punished "on the principle of an eye for an eye" (45). Foreign Minister Shaikh Sabah al-Ahmad, dismissing the Iranian accusations, laconically stated that the Kuwaiti assistance extended to Iraq was not a secret and was known to all (46).

It was Iraq which, with nine recorded high-level visits over the period under consideration, approached the Kuwaitis, rather than the reverse (see App. III). Much was made of Kuwaiti support in the Iraqi press (47). But the question of the border and the Kuwaiti islands again marred the relationship, though officially the matter was played down. Iraq was aware that the Kuwaiti government wanted to obtain a final border demarcation as soon as possible, and again started in this period to use this issue so as to win concessions on Warba and Bubiyan. In his long interview with **Al-Watan** of 3 May 1984, Saddam denied that Iraq had any problems with Kuwait, and insisted that official relations were "excellent" (**mumtaza**). Iraq, he stated, "has been always and still is ready to demarcate the borders with Kuwait"; the matter could be settled "when the atmosphere is right for such a move". The atmosphere, no doubt, would be right when the Kuwaitis agreed to his suggestion that Warba and Bubiyan or part of them be leased to Iraq for a period of 20 years. It is interesting, though, to note that the demand had come down from the original 90 years (48). The following Iraqi visits certainly touched upon this matter, although Tariq Aziz denied that the objective of his July 1984 visit was to rent the islands (49). Kuwait too, strongly denied that Iraq had officially asked for a lease in return for a border settlement (50). These denials were necessary so as to avoid serious embarrassment, since the Kuwaiti government knew that it would never agree to give up any part of the islands. Shaikh Saad's visit to Baghdad (on Iraq's invitation) resulted in little more than an intention to "study pending border issues" and, reportedly, to resume "study" of the water-provision project and the linking of the electricity grids (51). Saadun Shakir came to Kuwait shortly afterwards on a follow-up visit (52). But on the whole, Shaikh Saad is reported to have found his trip to Baghdad "quite disappointing" - whether or not it is true (as rumoured) that Saddam told him that his government recognised Kuwait's independence "despite the fact that the Iraqi people are against it" (53).

An **Observer** report that Iraqi troops had crossed the border in late November, and that anti-aircraft guns were installed in a disputed area, was denied by Kuwait (54). While evidence on this specific contention is difficult to come by, it is clear that the border question remained a serious irritant for Kuwaiti-Iraqi relations. It was equally clear, that Kuwait would never give in on the matter of the islands. After Shaikh Saad's Baghdad visit, Rafsanjani had issued an unambiguous warning:

> I am just telling the rulers of Kuwait not to play with fire (...) I say right now to Kuwait and the (GCC) member countries that if we were to capture that island from Iraq tomorrow, Kuwait would have no territorial claim there (55).

Kuwaits determination to retain sole control over Warba and Bubiyan was reflected in the installation of defences on the islands, such that Bubiyan in particular became "a military island equipped with anti-aircraft guns" (56).

As had held true in previous periods, Kuwaiti public opinion appeared to be firmly on the Iraqi side, with less reservations than the government. One indication of this was the appeal by private interests that Iraq be included in the GCC (an appeal which was ignored in official quarters) (57). Another was the attitude of the National Assembly. On 9 April 1985 the Assembly declared its support for Iraq's right to self-defence, and stressed that Kuwait "and our Arab people in Iraq are

linked   to   one   fate   and   destiny"   (58).   In   1984,   the
Assembly's   finance   committee   for   the   third   time   voted   to
cut   off   aid   to   Syria   for   its   support   of   Iran   against   a
fellow-Arab   country.   As   before,   the   votes   of   the   cabinet
reversed   the   balance   in   the   full   assembly,   but   the   level
of   aid   was   substantially   lowered   (59).   In   1985,   support
for   further   reduction   or   cancellation   of   the   aid   appeared
to   grow   even   stronger,   but   in   July   of   that   year,   the
National   Assembly   settled   for   a   compromise   with   the
government: the   annual   KD   100   million   subsidy   to   the
frontline   states   was   cancelled   but   foreign   assistance
funds   at   the   government's   disposal   were   raised   from   KD
80   million ,   to   KD   150   million,   which   the   government
could   grant   at   its   discretion   to   "Arab   and   friendly
states"   (60).   Circumstantial   evidence   for   the   anti-Syrian
bias   in   these   developments   can   be   found   in   the   increasing
Syrian   irritation.   Kuwait,   on   10   June   1985,   protested   to
Syria   over   anti-Kuwaiti   demonstrations   in   Damascus
against   Kuwait's   support   for   Iraq;   the   following   day,
Syria   recalled   its   ambassador   after   the   reported
deportation   of   several   Syrians   from   Kuwait   (61).   The
bitterness   towards   Iraq   and   the   lingering   suspicion   which
KUTSCHERA   in   **The   Middle   East**   reports   (62),   therefore,
seem   to   have   been   confined   mainly   to   the   official
quarters   and   a   minority   among   the   public.

Relations with the other Gulf states

The   other   Gulf   states   maintained   their   neutrality.
Neither   the   UAE   nor   Qatar   gave   any   further   aid.   They   did
join   Kuwait   and   Saudi   Arabia   in   strongly   condemning   the
Iranian   raids   on   Gulf   shipping,   without   mentioning   Iraqi
activities,   but   this   primarily   expressed   their   desire   to
protect   their   own   rights.   The   shooting   down   by   the   Saudi
airforce   of   the   Iranian   aircraft   on   5   June   1984   was   only
welcomed   very   cautiously;   a   Qatari   newspaper   even   called
it   "a   regrettable   incident".   Only   in   the   Bahraini   press
was   the   Saudi   action   applauded   wholeheartedly   (63),
reflecting   Bahrain's   reliance   on   Saudi   aerial   protection.

Iran   stepped   up   its   courting   of   the   UAE,   to   some   effect.
Two   Iranian   trade   attaches   were   posted   to   the   UAE,   one
based   at   the   embassy   in   Abu   Dhabi,   the   other   at   the
consulate-general   in   Dubai.   Interest   was   expressed   by   the
UAE   government   for   expanding   agricultural   cooperation
with   Iran   (64).   In   response   to   Velayati's   visit   to   the
UAE   after   his   December   talks   with   Saud   al-Faysal,   the   UAE
Minister   of   State   for   Foreign   Affairs   Rashid   al-Nu'aimi
went   to   Tehran   at   the   end   of   that   month.   On   the   occasion
of   this   visit,   Majlis   Speaker   Hashemi   Rafsanjani   stressed

that Iran did not realistically expect cooperation, but that neutrality on the part of the Gulf states would be acceptable; the UAE however, were singled out for praise for having expressed more positive views on Iran than other Gulf states. Al-Nu'aimi called the visit "a success" and invited Rafsanjani to visit the UAE (65).

Differing trends within the federation, however, were still in evidence. Abu Dhabi did not acquire the same ties with Iran as Dubai and Sharjah. The 'business as usual' attitude of the latter two was criticized by Tariq Aziz as "disgraceful" and as contravening "national standards" (66), which indicates that Abu Dhabi was still perceived as sympathetic to Iraq. The feelings of the **Al-Nihayyan** were no doubt similar to those expressed by a UAE diplomat quoted in **The Middle East**: "We stand with the Arabs, but this does not mean we want to commit suicide" (67). Mindful of Iraqi 'change-oriented activities' in the past, the Abu Dhabi ruling family did not want to offend Iraq too directly. Rumours that the UAE (read Abu Dhabi) was 'buying off' Iran (68), appear unfounded.

It is interesting to note that the Al-Maktum of Dubai towards the end of this period also appeared to be trying to manoeuvre away from Iraq's anger. After the November 1985 GCC Summit in Muscat, Shaikh Muhammad bin Rashid, the federal Minister of Defence and generally recognised as the real strong man of the Emirate after Shaikh Rashid, stated that the "GCC countries will not draw away from Iraq , because we are all Arabs together"; this certainly did not imply an anti-Iranian stance, because after all, he pointed out, Iran is also Muslim. But, coming from Shaikh Muhammad, the statement indicates that Dubai aligned itself at least to some degree with the federal and GCC position on the war. He made a point of denying that Dubai's trade with Iran was helping that country's war effort (69). Iraq for its part also appeared to soften its attitude towards Dubai. The trade mission which was sent to the emirate in October 1985 – the first since the start of the war – was evidently politically relevant (70).

In addition to visiting Saudi Arabia and Kuwait, Izzat Ibrahim, accompanied by a high-level delegation, also went to the UAE and the other small Gulf states in August 1984 (see App.III), delivering messages from Saddam Hussein to all the heads of state. Contrary to the reception which the delegation was given in Kuwait and Saudi Arabia, however, the response in the lower Gulf was restrained (71). Bahrain, Qatar and the UAE also

received, a little later, an official Iranian delegation
(72). The position of the lower Gulf states was expressed
with   typical   frankness   by   Sultan Qabus of Oman
in interviews with the Egyptian   newspapers **Al-Ahram** and
Al-Musawwar. He acknowledged Iraq's positive response to
peace   initiatives   and   implies   that   "our   brothers in
Iran" should be equally responsive. But, he warned:

> we   must not do anything   that   will   have   future
> negative effects   on   us ...   Our problem in the
> Gulf is that Iraq believes   -   and   perhaps it is
> partly right in its view - that Arab duty dictates
> that we should support it without reservations and
> regardless   of the consequences. At the same time,
> Iran believes   we   are   not   qualified   to play a
> mediating   role   because   of our Arab affiliation,
> despite our efforts to   adopt   objective   views on
> this futile conflict   (73).

Attempting   to   withdraw   even further   into   a   neutral
shelter, Qabus in his opening speech to the November 1985
GCC Summit gave not the   slightest hint of favouring Iraq
over Iran. Indeed, after it was   pointed   out to him that
the   final   communique   had still implicitly taken Iraq's
side and criticised Iran, he went so far as to say : "The
GCC communique was a   GCC   affair   but   one which had the
same meaning as mine - it does not contain a criticism of
either side" (74).

In conclusion, therefore, it appears   that   the   southern
Gulf states,   gently   coached along by Iran, had come to
accept by the   end   of   this   period   that neutrality was
their   best option and might even help provide   a   better
outlook for peaceful resolution of the conflict. Iraq had
come to acquiesce in this reality. Collectively, however,
in the   framework   of   the GCC, the southern Gulf states
still   tilted   towards   Iraq. Due to   the   understanding
stance   adopted   by   the   Iraqi   government,   moreover,
possible   strain   on the relationship   between   Iraq   and
these Gulf states was avoided.

NOTES TO CHAPTER VI

1.   Both the GCC Foreign Ministers and the Arab League in emergency meetings after the May attacks on Saudi and Kuwaiti tankers, strongly condemned the "Iranian aggresion". On 21 May the GCC announced it was seeking a UN Security Council meeting on the issue. The Security Council Resolution which was adopted on 1 June condemned the attacks but did not mention Iran by name as the GCC had asked. See KEESING'S 1984, p. 33058.

2.   KEESING'S, 1985, p. 33370

3.   SPA despatch 17-3-1984; **MEED**, 16-4-1984

4.   Tehran home service on 20-6-1984. quoted in **SWB** ME/

5.   **SWB** ME/7872/A/3, 11-2-1985

6.   IRNA , 14-2-1985

7.   **SWB**, ME/7184/A/9, 30-11-1984; and ME/7905/A/6, 21-3-1985. The Ministers in the March 1985 statement affirmed the GCC's "full solidarity with Iraq in preserving the sovereignty, safety and integrity of its territory".

8.   See further; and i.a. **MEES**, 10-6-1985, p. C2; **SWB** ME/7970/A/1, 6-6-2985.

9.   **SWB**, ME/8001/A/1, 12-7-1985

10. See **MEI**, 13-9-1985 and 27-9-1985.

11. **SWB**, ME/8099/i, 4-11-1985

12. **SWB**, ME/8048/A/1-2, 5-9-1985

13. **SWB**, ME/8102/A/4, 7-11-1985

14. See for instance **SWB**, ME/8106/A/4, 12-11-1985.

15. **SWB**, ME/8111/A/5, 18-11-1985

16. **SWB**, ME/8107/i, 13-11-1985

17. **Al-Watan**, 3-5-1985

18. **MEES**, 30-7-1984, p. D2

19. GHAREEB, 1986, p. 79

20. See i.a. KEESING'S, 1984,   pp. 33056-33059;   1985, p.
33560; **Time**, 26-3-1984, p. 15; 28-5-1984; 4-6-1984;
18-6-1984; 9-7-1984; 16-7-1984; HIRO, 1984, p. 13; **MEI**,
18-5-1984, pp. 6-7; **MEED**, 4-5-1984; 11-5-1984; **The
Guardian**, 4-6-1984; **ST**, 3-6-1984; and later press reports
(The **Guardian, The Times, Time, FT**).

21. **MEED**, 4-5-1984; 11-5-1984; **MEI**, 18-5-1984

22. **MEED**, 11-5-1984

23. **Al-Watan**, 3-5-1984;   **MEED**, 11-5-1984

24. **MEI**, 18-5-1984

25. **SWB** ME/7630/A/10, 30-4-1984

26. QNA dispatch, 19-5-1984

27. **ST**, 17-3-1985

28. KEESING'S, 1984, p. 33058

29. Quoted by **SWB** A/1, 4-7-1984.

30. **NYT**, 21-6-1984; DS, 22-6-1984

31. SPA dispatch of 8-8-1984; BO, 9-8-1985

32. See i.a. **SWB** ME/7956/A/2-6,   20-5-1985; ME/7957/A/2,
22-5-1985; also SPA dispatch 19-5-1985 (from Tehran).

33. See **MEI**, 13-9-1985 and 27-9-1985; **ST**, 22-9-1985; **The
Guardian**, 25-9-1985 and 26-9-1985.

34. **MEI**, 13-9-1985

35. Interview in **MEES**, 30-7-1984, p. D2.   Also SPA
dispatches, 13,14-6-1984; BO, 9-8-1984; INA quoted by
REUTER dispatch 9-8-1984.

36. **SWB**, ME/8124/A/2, 3-12-1985. Possibly, the attack
was a response to a Saudi-backed anti-Shi'a campaign in
Lebanon and Pakistan.

37. See **SWB**, ME/8130/A/5-8, 10-12-1985; ME/8131/A/3,
11-12-1985;   ME/8132/A/3-4,   12-12-1985;   **MEED**,
14-12-1985.

38. See note 12.

39. DS, 17-5-1984; KEESING'S, 1984, p. 33058

40. **SWB** ME/7961/A/1, 27-5-1985

41. See **SWB**, ME/7987/A/2, 26-6-1985; ME/8028/A/9, 13-8-1985; and press reports of August and September 1985.

42. SWB, ME/7697/A/4, 17-7-1984

43. Carried by KUNA, quoted by QNA, 5-8-1984.

44. **Al-siyasa**, 18-8-1985

45. SWB, ME/8043/A/1-2, 30-8-1985

46. SWB, ME/8050/A/5, 6-9-1985

47. See for instance **BO**, 6-8-1984.

48. **Al-Watan**, 3-5-1984

49. QNA dispatch 9-7-1984

50. **MEED**, 10-8-1984; **Gulf Mirror**, 15-8-1984.

51. SWB, ME/7806/7, 21-11-1984; ME/7804/A/3, 19-11-1984; **MEED**, 21-9-1984

52. SWB, ME/7806/i, 21-11-1984

53. **ME**, May 1985, p. 18

54. DS, 5-12-1984; **SWB**, ME/7816/A/6, 3-12-1984

55. SWB, ME/7803/i, 17-11-1984

56. **Al-Watan**, 2-12-1984; Defense Minister Shaikh Salem Al-Sabah in interview: **SWB**, ME/7908/A/3, 25-3-1985.

57. **EIU QER Iraq**, 1984, 2, p. 9

58. SWB, ME/7922/A/15, 11-4-1985

59. OTAQUI, 1985, p. 129

60. **The Arab Gulf Journal**, November 1985, pp. 89-90

61. **MEJ**, Autumn 1985, p. 802

62. **ME**, May 1984, p. 18

63. Press reactions cited in **MEI**, 15-6-1984.

64. See **MEED**, 31-8-1984, p. 38; **Khaleej Times**, 29-4-1984; **SWB**, ME/7564/A/1, 11-2-1984 (Iranian condolences on the murder of the UAE ambassador in Paris); **SWB**, ME/W 1281/A/3, 3-4-1984; **SWB**, ME/7850/A/9, 16-1-1985; and the reports by David HIRST in **the Guardian**, 1-8-1984 and Chris KUTSCHERA in **ME**, May 1985, p. 18.

65. **SWB**, ME/8144/A/8-9, 31-12-1985; **MEED**, 4-1-1986

66. Tariq Aziz in interview with **Akhbar al-Yaum**, 18-8-1984; **MEED**, 31-8-1984.

67. **ME**, May 1985, p. 18

68. The Guardian, 1-8-1984 (HIRST's article)

69. **MEED**, 23-11-1985

70. **MEED**, 12-10-1985

71. KUNA dispatch 7-8-1984; SPA dispatches 5,6-8-1984; REUTER dispatches of 5,6-8-1984

72. **SWB** ME/7850/A/9, 16-1-1985; ME/7845/A/6, 10-1-1985; ME/7846/A/6, 11-1-1985

73. Quote **from Al-Musawwar**, 5-4-1985. Other interview (**Al-Ahram**) quoted in **SWB**, ME/7855/A/1, 22-1-1985.

74. **MEED**, 14-12-1985; **SWB**, ME/8100/A/1, 5-11-1985

CHAPTER SEVEN

POLITICAL ATTITUDES AND RELATIONSHIPS AFTER 9 FEBRUARY
1986

In an offensive which started on 9 February 1986, the
Iranian army crossed the Shatt al-Arab on to the Fao
peninsula. It captured Fao itself and a considerable part
of the peninsula, which controls Iraq's access to the
Gulf and is only separated from Kuwait's Bubiyan island
by the Khor al-Abdallah (see maps). The shock was
eventually absorbed, but not without Iraq conceding
serious losses of troops and territory in a crucial area.
Moreover, this Iraqi setback came at a time when oil
prices plummeted to below $ 15 per barrel, reversing the
previously improving trend in the country's finances (see
Ch. VIII). On 25 February Iran launched another offensive
in the north, where it received some support from Kurdish
tribes in Iraq (1). Although Iraq could subsequently
claim some successes in the north, its vulnerability was
again highlighted. The serious nature of the threat to
Iraq was emphasised when Iran massed troops along the
southern front during the months which followed. In early
June Khomeini called for total mobilisation (2). A
concomitant of this new phase in the war, with
implications for the Gulf states, was the further
escalation of the tanker war. In the first three months
of the year alone, there were 28 confirmed hits, as
against 40 for the whole of 1985 (3).

Each of the six GCC states issued statements condemning
Iran's offensive. On 12 February the Arab League Gulf War
follow-up committee, which included the Foreign Ministers
of Saudi Arabia and Kuwait, undertook a supportive vist
to Baghdad. In the Security Council discussion a week
later, Saudi Arabia's criticism of Iran was backed by
Kuwait and Oman, in addition to Tunisia and Jordan. These
states called on Iran to listen to the "voice of reason"
(4). Tehran initially told the Gulf states "not to worry"
and said it would not expand the war to include them (5);
but in the face of the increased support for Iraq,
Iranian threats particularly to Kuwait and Saudi Arabia
grew. Majlis Speaker Hashemi Rafsanjani warned:

These countries should always remember that we are
now on their border ... Iran will no longer accept
that your ports should receive arms shipments for
Iraq, that your roads should be used to strengthen
the Iraqi army, and that Iraqi oil should pass
across your territory. (6)

Four days later, President Khamenei stated: "Some
countries admit they sell oil for Iraq. Everyone will
accept, that, if we make the decision one day, we can
confiscate the oil sold for Iraq" (7).

But the communique issued after the GCC Foreign
Ministers' meeting in Riyadh, 1 - 3 March, made it clear
that the Iranian offensive and subsequent threats, rather
than reinforcing the growing trend of neutrality, had in
fact moved the Gulf states closer to Iraq. The Six
affirmed their capability to defend themselves, referring
in particular to the new "Peninsula Shield" rapid
deployment force. The full text of the communique is
reproduced in English in Appendix VII. The Council
condemned the occupation of Fao as a violation of Iraq's
sovereignty and international conventions, criticised
Iranian threats to GCC states as threatening the
stability of the region, affirmed its adherence to the
principle of peaceful coexistence, and once more praised
Iraq for its willingness to settle the conflict
peacefully. On 5 March, the GCC Chiefs of Staff met in
Riyadh, reportedly in connection with contingency plans
for the deployment of the 3000-strong Saudi-led
"Peninsula Shield" force in the vicinity of Kuwait (8).

The Iranian leadership professed amusement at the Gulf
states' threats and warned that Iran would "never
hesitate to respond decisively to their childish plots",
but President Khamenei and others still stuck to the line
that Iran did not want to spread the war. In tune with
its previous approach, the Iranian government still tried
to build bridges to the Gulf states, or at least to split
them. Saudi Arabia and Kuwait were singled out in a
declaration by Kamal Kharrazi of Iran's War Information
Headquarters, as the only two GCC states hostile to Iran.
Kharrazi suggested that Iran still hoped that even these
two states might stop supporting Saddam, since, he
claimed, "there is a difference between what they say in
public and what they tell us in private" (9). Such
statements, however, probably offer a truer image of
Iran's tactics than of the Gulf states' attitudes. The
Gulf states acted together in insisting, along with Iraq,
that the Gulf War be included in the agenda of the Arab

Summit proposed after the US raid on Libya in April 1986
- even though this meant, given the strong opposition
from Iran, Libya and Syria, that the Summit failed to
materialise.

There were, however, differences in how the individual
Gulf states reacted to the new situation obtaining after
9 February.

Relations with Saudi Arabia

When the Iranian army attacked on 9 February, both Izzat
Ibrahim and the Iraqi Oil Minister Ahmad Qasim Taqi were
in Riyadh. They stayed there until the next day, holding
talks with Defence Minister Prince Sultan and Shaikh
Yamani. Izzat also met with Crown Prince Abdullah and
probably King Fahd (10). The official subject of the
talks was the developments in the oil markets - at that
stage indeed of critical importance. To a certain extent,
the visit's timing was a coincidence, since the main
assault began after the delegation had left Baghdad.
However, the Iraqi government must already have known
that an attack was likely, partly because of Iraq's
relative success in hampering Iran's oil exports. Almost
as soon as news of the attack had become public, on 10
February, the Saudi Council of Ministers issued a
statement through Information Minister Ali al-Sha'ir,
which was quoted in the reports of the Saudi Press Agency
and again the next day in the Saudi newspapers. The
Council "deeply regretted the new Iranian offensive
against Iraq especially at a time when intensive Arab
efforts are being made to bring peace and stability to
the region", and reacted "with pain and sorrow", because
the attack could threaten the security of the enire
region and would inevitably result in heavy human and
material losses. The Council referred to "Iraq's
perpetual and repeated favourable peace responses since
the third Islamic summit conference held in Taif in
January 1981" and hoped that "Iran would finally respond
to the repeated calls by the UN Security Council, the
Arab and Islamic states and all peace-loving countries of
the world". Iran should "understand that peace is the
only solution" (11).

On 12 February, the Saudi Press Agency reported that King
Fahd had telephoned Saddam Hussein "to inquire about the
latest offensive", adding that "President Saddam
expressed profound gratitude" for the King's "brotherly
sentiments". In the above-mentioned Security Council
discussions of 19 February, Saudi Arabia urged the

Council to take "a decisive stand not only on the escalation of hostilities but also on obstruction to the UN moves to put an end to the war" (12), thus clearly condemning Iran.

Saudi criticism of Iran was thus expressed clearly in the state-controlled press. This constituted a significant change. Up to January, the war had been reported in a 'neutral' manner, with reports taken from international press agencies. After the attack reports reverted to conveying mainly the Iraqi version of events, and quoting pro-Iraqi voices such as those of Egypt and Jordan. Commentaries in editorials,however, tended to be less aggressive in tone than those found in Kuwaiti newspapers (see below): Iran was berated for its responsibility in the flare-up, but in a very restrained, sometimes even conciliatory way. Also, Iran was still given a hearing, albeit a less prominent one than that given to Iraq (13).

On the one hand, then, the Saudi leadership did not wish to present an unnecessarily aggressive front, always hoping to restrain Iran from attacking it. There was a willingness to develop bilateral relations further, as long as that did not imply giving up more crucial interests. On the other hand, the Kingdom's actual support for Iraq was in no way affected. Indeed, contrary to previous expectations, the oil-swap arrangement was continued, and the projects relating to the transport of Iraqi oil over Saudi territory to the Red Sea coast proceeded without any sigificant hitch – even though these were precisely the main elements over which the Iranian leadership attacked and threatened the Al-Saud (see Ch. VIII). Further evidence of Iraqi-Saudi understanding is provided by their oil policies, which placed them (and the other Arab Gulf producers) in the camp opposite to that of Iran. Their attempt to push up production, leading in the short term to depressed prices, was seen by the Iranians as an anti-Iranian plot (Ch. VIII, C). It is telling, too, that no less than four high-level contacts took place (not counting Fahd's telephone call to Saddam) over the two weeks which followed the 9 February assault. Prince Saud al-Faysal conferred with the Iraqi President in Baghdad on three occasions – twice accompanied by Kuwait's Shaikh Sabah al-Ahmad, in the framework of the Arab League follow-up committee (see Appendix III) which was still trying to restore ties between Syria and Iraq.

Relations with Kuwait

The shift in Kuwait's public attitude was even more pronounced. On 11 February the government and the National Assembly issued a joint statement, stressing that both condemned the "frequent Iranian attempts to occupy some Iraqi land and jeopardise the stability of the sisterly country" (14), a statement quoted repeatedly in all the media. It was, indeed, Kuwait which was most directly threatened by Iran's latest moves. The Defence Minister, Shaikh Salim Al-Sabah, expressed the Emirate's refusal to give in to the Iranian threats when he stated on 23 February: "If Iran would choose to be our enemy, we are ready for that"; two days later he elaborated further: "our armed forces stand firm in their resolve to defend the country in the face of Iranian threats" (15). A striking change took place in the reporting of the war on the government-controlled radio and television. Whereas up to then, for instance, few pictures of the fighting had reached Kuwaiti viewers, Kuwaiti Television now began giving lengthy reports on frontline events, showing minutes-long excerpts of the Iraqi Television's filmed reports on Iraq's 'victories'.

The comparatively free press gave unambiguous support to Iraq and Saddam Hussein, both in the English- and the Arabic-language newspapers. For an outside observer, the volume and intensity of accusations against Iran, and the near-total identification with the pronouncements and aims of the Iraqi regime, were quite overwhelming. The first reactions, on 11 February, spoke about the plans of the Iraqi military command to end the war once and for all "by paralysing the Iranian military machine" (**Al-Qabas**); claimed that "there is no difference between (American) fleets and planes which threaten Libya in the Mediterranean, and the human flood threatening Iraqi land and waters" (**Al-Ra'y al-'Amm**); were confident of Iraq's good military position and the Iraqis' loyalty to their regime (**Al-siyasa**); and praised Iraq's steadfastness against the Iranian assault, pledging the support of the Arab Gulf states (**Al-Anbaa'**). During the days which followed, **Al-Anbaa'** rejected Iran's threats over Bubiyan and Kuwaiti aid to Iraq, suggesting that it was obviously Iraq rather than Iran which wished Kuwait well. The paper condemned Arab countries supporting Iran, warning them they would soon find that "they are digging the grave for Arab dignity and destiny" (16). **Al-Watan** accused Iran of fighting an insane war for a lost cause, and of serving US interests; it called the Iranian

leadership "warlords" feeding the "death machine" (17).
Al-Qabas spoke about Iran's "resounding defeat" and
lamented the Iranian stubbornness and arrogance (18).
Al-Siyasa termed Iran's insistence on continuing the war
"political madness". Iran, the paper said, "has become a
heavy burden on the whole area" and should "learn a
lesson from the fate of Hitler who tried to dominate
Europe and dreamed of conquering the world" (19). The
English-language press repeated all these condemnations
of Iran and praise for Iraq, adding to them in the
process. Thus, for instance, the 11 February editorial in
the **Arab Times** concluded by warning Iran that

> it will be gravely mistaken if it thinks for a
> moment that there is anyone who can negotiate or
> bargain over President Saddam Hussein's leadership,
> or even think of such a possibility. This is
> because Saddam Hussein is not for Iraq alone, but
> is a great barrier that halts the risks and dangers
> surrounding this region, dangers which Iran is
> always trying to export.

To conclude this list of examples from the pro-Iraqi
avalanche in the Kuwaiti press, the **Kuwait Times**
editorial on 12 February described the Iranian insistence
on pursuing the war as contrary to international law or
any other law, canon, custom or practice, and " wholly
repugnant to the spirit, theory and practice of Islam".
The article went on:

> This mindless resort to reactivate a dormant war
> cannot be without some compelling motivation.
> Possibly it has something to do with the completion
> of seven years of rule by the present leadership.
> As is normal, such anniversaries are occasions when
> leaders and governments are expected to tell their
> people about their achievements and victories. As
> it happens, the people in Tehran had precious
> little to show for the tumultuous and blood-stained
> seven years of the revolutionary era. A diversion
> was needed. Hence the return to attack... Iran's
> onslaught on Iraq is a fact ... Let there be
> decisive action by all concerned. And that means
> the whole world ... This is war. It has been
> restarted by a party. That party should be
> subjected to international discipline. The matter
> is as simple as that. Let it be seen as such and
> dealt with as such.

Among large parts of Kuwaiti public opinion, the Iranian
offensive gave a new twist to suspicion of Shi'ites in

the country, fanned by events such as the assassination
attempt on the Amir and the bombings of two seaside
cafes. The support for Iraq as a bulwark against the
Iranian (Shi'i) threat, so loudly voiced in the press,
can at least in part be seen as an extension of that
suspicion. The strongly pro-Iraqi feelings among many
Kuwaitis at this time are illustrated further by two news
items which appeared in the Kuwaiti press. It was
reported in February that one Kuwaiti had given the
equivalent of $ 645,000 to Iraq towards the cost of the
war (20); and in April that, in all, more than KD 153
million ($ 525 million) had been collected in Kuwait for
the same cause (21).

It is clear, then, that the Kuwaiti government, with
considerable backing in public opinion, took an
unequivocally pro-Iraqi stand from the start of this
period. This was prompted both by the directly military
threat to Iraq and Kuwait, and by consideration of Iraq's
new financial difficulties in the wake of the slide in
oil prices. Iraqi-Kuwaiti understanding was reflected in
cooperation in the economic field : Kuwait agreed to
continue supplying oil from the Neutral Zone on behalf of
Iraq; and a vital project to bring Iraqi gas to Kuwait
was completed, promising Kuwait fulfilment of its gas
requirements, and Iraq some $ 500 million in extra annual
income. As indicated, Kuwait's oil policies put it in
Saudi Arabia's camp, and were not contested by Iraq.
These policies brought harsh criticism from Iran, and may
even have provided the cause for the June bombings of
some oil installations by saboteurs (22), but Kuwait's
stance remained one of defiance.

Relations with the other Gulf states

As indicated, the other Gulf states also condemned the
Iranian offensive; their common stand in favour of Iraq
was reflected in the GCC Foreign Ministers' communique of
3 March. But compared to the attitudes adopted by Kuwait
or even Saudi Arabia, they remained restrained. The
Bahraini **Akhbar al-Khalij** commented that the "Iranian
leaders commit a great folly if they think that by
rejecting peace calls to end the war they can bring Iraq
to its knees" (23). In the case of the UAE, the picture
was, as usual, somewhat confused. The press, largely
self-censoring and differing according to the Emirate
where a paper is published, offers conflicting evidence.
In no case, however, was criticism of Iran as pronounced
as in Kuwait. The English-language **Emirates News** stuck to
neutral reporting. **Al-Bayan** (Dubai) gave both the Iraqi

and Iranian versions of events on the front; its editorials, though lamenting the flare-up, did not explicitly condemn Iran, taking pains instead always to mention both countries' names or neither. The only implicit criticism was contained in a phrase in the 13 February editorial, stating that it was unacceptable for one party to occupy land of the other. **Al-Ittihad** (Abu Dhabi) expressed the opinion that the new Iranian-initiated phase in the war was detrimental to the whole region (24). The most overtly critical reactions after the initial offensive came from the Sharjah-based **Al-Khalij**. In its 12 February editorial, the paper intimated that no Arab worthy of his name could accept occupation of any Arab territory, and wondered aloud where the Iranian government thought these kinds of events were leading, and what its aims could possibly be in its persistent efforts to occupy Iraqi soil. Iran, it stressed, had no right to interfere in Iraq's affairs. The paper appealed to Iran to respond to Iraq's willingness to end the war. Similar appeals and implicit condemnation of Iran were carried in later editorials.

– – – –

In conclusion, the combined effect of sharply dropping oil prices and the renewed Iranian aggression after 9 February jolted the Gulf states into a more clearly pro-Iraqi attitude. Oman was the least eager to give up its as-neutral-as-possible shelter, while trends in the United Arab Emirates still went in different directions. Bahrain and Qatar moved with Saudi Arabia towards a more assertative stand, though stopping well short of the Saudi position and not supplying material assistance to Iraq. Saudi Arabia continued to effectively fully support Iraq, while at the same time trying to salvage any bilateral detente with Iran which would still be possible. Kuwait gave up even that conciliatory front and, in the face of direct Iranian verbal and military threats, unequivocally took Iraq's side. Iraq for its part, saw its dependence on its wealthy neighbours Kuwait and Saudi Arabia increase again, which only reinforced its accommodating attitude towards these states, as was evident in its taking the Gulf producers' side in the OPEC split (see Ch. VIII, C).

NOTES TO CHAPTER VII

1. FT, 20-5-1986

2. See **MEED**, 3-5-86; 10-5-86; 17-5-86; 24-5-86; 31-5-86.

3. **MEES**, 7-4-1986

4. See **MEES**, 17-2-1986; **KT**, 13-2-1986.

5. **Jordan Times**, 24-2-1986

6. **MEES**, 3-3-1986

7. ibid.

8. **MEES**, 10-3-1986

9. **MEED**, 29-3-1986; **MEES**, 10-3-1986; 17-3-1986

10. EN, 10-2-1986; **GN**, 10-2-1986; Khaleej Times, 10-2-1986

11. **Arab News**, 11-2-1986

13. See the February issues of **Arab News, Al-Riyadh, Saudi Gazette, Al-Madina,** and other newspapers.

14. **KT**, 12-2-1986; **MEES**, 17-2-1986

15. Quoted in **MEES**, 3-3-1986

16. **Al-Anbaa'**, 12-2-1986; 15-2-1986

17. **Al-Watan**, 12-2-1986

18. **Al-Qabas**, 12-2-1986

19. **Al-siyasa**, 12--1986

20. **MEED**, 1-3-1986

21. **MEED**, 19-4-1986

22. **The Guardian**, 19-6-1986

23. **Akhbar al-Khalij**, 12-2-1986

24. **Al-Ittihad,** 12-2-1986

————

CHAPTER EIGHT

ECONOMIC AND SOCIO–CULTURAL RELATIONS

A. Aid

The Gulf states started giving financial aid to Iraq in
the autumn of 1980. Except for Kuwait, no precise figures
have ever been made public, but educated 'guesstimates'
are possible on the basis of press reports, information
from banking and other well-informed sources, and taking
account of Iraqi national accounts and the financial
situation of the Gulf states (see Tables 1 - 10 in
Appendix V). Commercial loans will not be covered in this
section, although some of those have had a political
element (see section E. 4). Consideration will be
restricted to government-to-government loans and grants,
and counterpart oil sales, the extent of which is better
documented.

1. Financial Aid

Kuwait appears to have given three loans, each of $ 2
billion. The first was given in the autumn of 1980, and
retroactively approved by the re-established National
Assembly in November 1981. The second was approved in
April 1981, the third in December 1981. The loans
were interest-free, without commission, and repayable
over 10 years (1). The Kuwaiti press reported in April
1981 that Iraq had asked for a $ 14 billion package from
Kuwait, Saudi Arabia, the UAE and Qatar (2). This was
denied by Iraqi Finance Minister Thamir Razzouki, who
also specifically denied having asked Kuwait for the
autumn 1980 loan. The ratification document of the latter
loan arrangement, however, was published in the Iraqi
Official Gazette; it stated explicitly that Iraq had
asked for the loan to "to help meet the burden of
repaying war damage" (3). There is no evidence of similar
disbursements from 1982 onwards. Abdellatif Yusuf
al-Hamad, then Finance Minister, confirmed in 1982 that
such aid had stopped, explaining that it was not possible
under the Kuwaiti political system to decide on such

disbursements   without   gaining   the   approval   of   the
National   Asembly   and   publishing   details   in   the   Official
Gazette (4).

The reports about the $ 14 billion package seem to have
been   well-founded,   and   apparently accurate at least as
far as the Kuwaiti share was concerned ($ 4 bn before the
Iraqi   request   for   the   third   loan).   The Saudi share was
put at $ 6 billion, and sources   close   to   Saudi Finance
Minister   Abalkhail   confirmed   that   the   Kingdom   had
pledged   between $ 4 and 6   billion (5).   Qatar's share
was reported to be $ 1   billion,   that   of   the UAE $ 3
billion.   There   is   no certainty about any earlier Saudi
disbursements, but it is unlikely that total Saudi aid by
April 1981 exceeded those $ 6 billion. In that month,
Razzouki   confirmed   that   Arab   loans   up   to   then   had
totalled $ 12 bilion (6). The approximate distribution of
that aid among the donors in April 1981   was probably:

Saudi Arabia	Kuwait	UAE	Qatar
$ 6 bn	$ 4 bn	$ 1-3 bn	$ 1 bn

During the rest of 1981,   as   indicated,   another $ 2 bn
from   Kuwait was forthcoming, and approximately another $
4 bn from Saudi Arabia (7). In a February 1983 interview,
Tariq Aziz put   the amount of aid received from the Gulf
states up to the   end   of   1981,   at   between $ 18 and 20
billion   (8).   This brings the probable approximate donor
distribution at the end of 1981 to:

Saudi Arabia	Kuwait	UAE	Qatar
$ 10 bn	$ 6 bn	$ 1-3 bn	$ 1 bn

In 1982 Iraq was reported   to   have asked for another $ 7
billion   (9).   Nothing   more was forthcoming from Kuwait,
nor, most likely, from   Qatar. There were reports that an
agreement had been   reached   between   the   GCC states and
Iraq at the Fez Summit, such that   the   bulk of the Iraqi
request   would   have been met by the Gulf states offering
another $ 6.5   billion   (10).   No   firm   evidence   is
available, but the   rumours   appear   consistent. It seems
that the UAE paid up another $ 1 bn or so. Certainly,
more aid was forthcoming from Saudi   Arabia, probably in
the region of $ 4 bn in   1982   (11).   Reports about new
Iraqi   requests   for   aid   in late 1982 (12) seem to have
been based on confusion, stemming   from Iraqi reiteration
of its pre-Fez requests, which obviously   remained valid.
It is certainly plausible that the Iraqi government would
have   repeated   and possibly raised these requests before
the November GCC   summit.   Saudi   Arabia favoured giving
more aid, but the matter was   left   as a bilateral issue,
indicating   the   unwillingness of the others to part with
further billions (13).   Saudi Arabia's positive response,
however, apparently materialised in   the   disbursement of

another $ 6 billion, reportedly made   available   over the
first half of 1983; consistent rumours to that effect are
confirmed by usually reliable sources (14).

At   the   end   of   1982,   therefore,   the   approximate
distribution per donor was:

Saudi Arabia	Kuwait	UAE	Qatar
$ 14 bn	$ 6 bn	$ 2-4 bn	$ 1 bn

The final Saudi $ 6 billion would have brought the Saudi
total to about $ 20 bn,   and   the overall total in direct
financial aid from the Gulf states to an approximate $ 29
- 31 billion. This is consistent with the Iraqi statement
at the end of 1982 that total aid so far amounted to not
more   than $ 25 billion (15). Exactly how these amounts
were   made   available is   not   clear,   but   most   of   the
contributions   probably followed   the   Kuwaiti   model   of
soft, medium   and   long   term   loans - although in effect
they may   amount   to grants. At least some $ 5 billion out
of the total were probably "goods   and   services" rather
than   actual   financial   disbursements (16). Included in
the overall total are   payments   to   Iraqi trade partners
such   as   France, and the sums (covering   the   difference
between Iraqi and   Saudi   oil   prices) which Saudi Arabia
paid to the Iraqi government for   the crude that was sold
to Iraqi clients during 1981 and 1982 (see section 2).

Some   sources   insist   that   further   financial   aid   was
forthcoming from 1983 onwards ($ 10 - 15 billion per year
according to EIU)(17); QUANDT, for instance, reports that
from the summer of 1983   money   started   coming in larger
quantities again, after hints from the US that   it   would
be   unwise   to stop aid to Iraq at that stage (18). There
is, however, no   firm   evidence   of such major aid flows,
apart from the oil counterpart   sales.   It is likely that
in some cases guarantees to some suppliers   of   Iraq were
given   in   case   of   payments deferrals, and Kuwait, like
other   countries   doing   business   with Iraq,   certainly
provided financing for some Kuwaiti   companies working in
Iraq. A report that Saudi Arabia   and   Kuwait   have   been
providing   partial   down   payments   to   providers of long
term loans (19) seems credible, considering the obviously
political decisions behind some of the 'commercial' loans
given   to   Iraq (see section   E).   Reliable   information
indicates that in at   least   some cases from 1983 through
1985 - involving British companies   - Kuwait has provided
down-payments of some 10 % of   the contracts' value. Even
by   the most generous calculations possible, however, all
this cannot have exceeded the $ 1-2 bn range annually; it
is in   fact   unlikely to have reached $ 1 bn, let alone a
yearly $ 10 bn or more.

Two other approaches to the question about the volume of
financial aid from the Gulf states to Iraq can be used.
One is to estimate the Iraqi needs, i.e. the gap between
expenditure and the sum of income, commercial loans, and
the drawing down of reserves, since the start of the war.
This is used by the proponents of the higher estimates of
aid-flows. However, the researcher's own conclusion from
just such calculations is that there is no need at all to
assume greater aid-flows than the one estimated above.
Data about Iraqi national accounts are difficult to come
by, often confidential, and vary from one source to
another; such data as are available, however, never
produce a gap larger than can be filled by the sum of the
combined export earnings, commercial loans and payments
deferrals, drawing down of reserves, the aid total
arrived at above, and the proceeds from oil swaps (to be
treated below). In Table 1 of Appendix V, the author's
estimates of this balance are presented (excluding the $
1bn in Euroloans obtained so far and the small loans from
the Islamic Development Bank and Arab institutions: see
section E 4). The financing gap at the end of 1985 would,
then, have amounted to at least $40 bn and perhaps as
much as $ 58 bn. Of this amount, over $ 9 bn were
accounted for by payments deferrals due to credit
agencies of OECD countries and some $ 6 bn was owed
directly to companies from those countries; roughly
another $ 9 bn had come from Kuwait's and Saudi Arabia's
oil counterpart sales (see section 2). Iraq, however,
probably left between $ 1 and $ 5 bn of its reserves
untouched. Incalculating these figures (see Table 1),
this leaves a financing gap at the end of 1985 of at
least $ 17 bn (the 'low case' of Table 1), but quite
possibly up to $ 39 bn ('high case'). It must be pointed
out that this equation does not take into account Soviet
and Eastern Bloc credit, about which no reliable data are
available, but which could well have amounted to between
$ 5 and $ 10 bn at the end of 1985. These figures are
easily squared with the researcher's earlier conclusions
about the amount of financial aid extended to Iraq by the
Gulf states.

The second approach consists in looking at the matter
from the side of the Gulf states: how much could they
afford to disburse, and what does the evidence about
transfers indicate ? Data about the latter would, if
anything, revise the figure drastically downward; but
they are scanty, and certainly do not cover the total.
Let us examine, then, the state of Saudi and Kuwaiti
finances and reserves (see App. V, Tables 2 - 10).

Saudi Arabia.

The Kingdom's oil revenues, peaking at $ 113.2 bn in 1981, were down to $ 28 bn in 1985 (20); estimates for 1986 go as low as $ 16 - 18 bn (21). SAMA figures about Saudi finances, covering 1981 - 1984, were revised in the spring of 1986, resulting in a much improved picture; pre- and post-revision figures are presented in table 4. It is not clear how credible the revised figures are, but they would bring the combined current account deficit over 1983 and 1984 down to approximately $ 34 bn, from c. $ 39 bn previously. The total 1981 - 1984 revision would mean that over that period there was a surplus of some $ 13 bn, rather than a $ 4 bn deficit. As for the volume and changes in the country's reserves, the May 1986 issue of IFS put total SAMA assets in 1982 at the equivalent of c. $ 282 bn, dropping by some $ 46 bn to $ 236 bn in 1984. Foreign assets over that period are listed as having dropped from c. $ 141 bn to c. $ 118 bn (caculated from figures in SR in table 5). These figures, particularly those for "total assets", appear much higher than generally accepted and probably include assets of some sort which are not usually included as part of SAMA's reserves. MUEHRING, after lengthy research in and outside SAMA, came up with a different set of figures (table 6): "total funds" as of April 1983 were put at $ 140 bn. $ 118 bn of these were interest-bearing foreign assets, a figure which dropped by almost $ 18 bn to just over $ 100 bn in August 1984.

SAMA's foreign assets at the end of 1985 were estimated at about $ 80 bn (22), which is consistent with the estimated 1985 current account deficit of at least $ 20 bn (23).

There is some discussion about the degree of liquidity of these assets. Liquidity is limited by the the rule that Saudi Riyals in circulation have to be covered by hard currency or - since 1982 - by short term US Treasury bills or notes (24). Limited liquidity is also inherent in the kinds of assets which SAMA holds, as is illustrated in table 6. SAMA includes its commitments to the IMF and the World Bank in its "assets", as well as billions' worth of soft loans and commitments mainly to Arab states; at least some of the Kingdom's assistance to Iraq is included (25). The Director of **Wharton**'s Middle East section in March 1986 put the fully liquid amount of Saudi assets at the end of 1985 at only $ 20 - 30 bn (25). If the IMF and World Bank commitments are counted as liquid, total liquid assets would then have come to $ 35 - 45 bn.

SAMA's 1986 upward revision of the current account
balance from 1981 through 1984 does not necessarily mean
that the estimates about SAMA's reserves have to be
revised upwards too; MUEHRING's data, for instance, are
not based on budget figures. This is equally true for
estimates of liquidity. Even if, as in one comment (27),
liquid assets are revised upward to c. $ 45 bn, the
picture remains rather grim. The most optimistic estimate
which has recently been made, putting liquid assets at
$ 60 bn, would still mean that Saudi Arabia under present
circumstances could only hold out for another 3 - 4 years
at most, without depleting its reserves (28). The most
pessimistic, based on **Wharton**'s estimate, has the
Kingdom's consumable reserves running out by the end of
1986. **MEED** reports a leading US bank's internal journal
as credibly estimating "usable assets" at c. $ 55 bn,
some of which, though, would be difficult to liquidise
(29).

In conclusion, considering (a) the quickly shrinking
volume of Saudi reserves, (b) their limited liquidity,
(c) the cost in terms of international reputation, of
withdrawing commitments to international organisations,
(d) the loss in commercial credibility that would result
from early withdrawals from long-term deposits and
investments; and (e) the great needs of the Treasury for
financing domestic expenditure (with big current account
deficits arising from 1983 onwards), it seems clear that
not much more would have been available for Iraq than the
figure we arrived at earlier. Seeing that Iraq was coping
adequately and was looking forward to an improved
financial position, the Saudis up to the end of 1985 had
no compelling reason to risk economic exhaustion and
international political and commercial loss of face.

Kuwait.

Kuwait's 1985 oil revenues of $ 9 bn were only half those
of the peak year 1980 (see table 2). The country's
balance of payments from 1983 to 1986 is given in table
8, indicating that although the surplus has dropped, a
surplus of $ 3.8 bn was still forecast for 1986. The
current account, inclusive of investment income (see
table 7), also remains in (shrinking) surplus. As shown
in table 10, Kuwaiti reserves in 1985 were still growing,
though slowly. The "State General Reserve" (SGR)
continued to contract, but this was offset by the
increase in the "Reserve Fund for Future Generations"
(RFFG). In fact, the annual replenishments of the RFFG
amounting to 10 % of the budget, have been taken from the

SGR for a few years now, and revenue-expenditure
shortfalls have been covered with SGR funds, sometimes
taking out more than was compensated for by new profit
and interest (30). Total Reserves at the end of 1985
stood at KD 24.13 bn ($ 85 bn). Of this, the SGR
accounted for KD 11.24 bn ($ 39 bn). By law, the RFFG
funds can not be touched until the beginning of the next
century. Some $ 12 bn out of the SGR's $ 39 bn, consist
of its Arab portfolio. Half of this is accounted for by
the loans to Iraq; another $ 0.8 bn by non-KFAED loans to
other Arab countries; and the rest is also mainly
illiquid. This leaves only the SGR's foreign portfolio
and its contributions to international organisations.
Taking into consideration the same concern for
international standing as in the Saudis' case, this
means, in **MEES'** assessment, that "for all practical
purposes only 2 % or KD 512 mn ($ 1.8 bn) of Kuwait's ...
nest-egg is available for current consumption purposes"
(31). Including less highly liquid assets, to which
access could be gained if deemed necessary, the estimate
of Kuwait's available reserves can be raised to c. $ 25
bn (32). Moreover, the law on the RFFG has recently been
proved less than sacrosanct, when it was argued that in a
case of exceptional need such as the Suq al-Manakh
crisis, it was acceptable to 'safeguard the future' by
dipping into the RFFG today. The same argument could
conceivably be used with regard to support for Iraq,
after 9 February 1986.

In conclusion, Kuwait appears to have been somewhat more
capable than Saudi Arabia to provide continuing financial
assistance; in Kuwait's case too, however, it was very
much a matter of political will. It is highly unlikely
that any further direct cash grants were made after the
initial $ 6 bn: the domestic and international political
and economic cost of further substantial dipping into the
reserves would no doubt have been considered too high, at
least upto the end of 1985.

- - - -

In 1986, an extra gap of between $ 15 - 19 bn was
expected in Iraq's financial balance, due to the sharp
drop in oil prices, the rise in war costs, and debt
servicing (which will probably amount to some $ 3 bn a
year (see table V-1). It is clear that Gulf states can
not cover all of this. As indicated above, the question
as to whether they will now decide, or have already
decided, to provide direct cash grants and possibly raise

other forms of financial assistance, is mainly a matter
of political will and their weighing of two evils. The
author believes that the political will exists, and that
consequently financial aid from Saudi Arabia and Kuwait
increased again in 1986 after a 3-year lapse, to a level
which will probably be maintained as long as Iraq remains
under acute financial and military pressure.

2. Oil Swaps

Official government-to-government arrangements for
counterpart oil sales by Saudi Arabia and Kuwait on
behalf of Iraq only began in 1983. Already in the fourth
quarter of 1980, however, Saudi Arabia had boosted its
output to produce some 440,000 b/d of "war relief" crude
to fulfil Iraq's oil supply contracts, in order for Iraq
not to run up penalties or lose its customers (33). This
oil was sold at the official Iraqi price - some $ 2 per
barrel more than the Saudi price - and, at least in 1981,
the difference was handed over to the Iraqi government
(34). The arrangement was apparently stopped in July 1981
(35). Then, in July 1982, a deal was struck between
Iraq's SOMO (**State Organisation for Marketing Oil
Products**) , **Mobil** (one of the **Aramco** partners) and
Mitsubishi. The latter corporation, representing three
other Japanese corporations, accepted oil, delivered by
Mobil, in part payment for Iraqi contracts. SOMO
undertook to pay Mobil the official price of $ 34 /b. The
arrangement covered 30,000 b/d in the 3rd quarter of
1982, and 40,000 b/d in the 4th. Although presumably the
Saudi government gave its agreement, it was not
officially involved. The deal presented simply a
facility, not aid (36).

From the beginning of 1983, however, Saudi Arabia and
Kuwait started providing crude for sale to Iraqi
customers and to parties willing to accept oil in
payment of contracts in or deliveries to Iraq. No
details are available as to who lifted the oil initially,
but the agreement was confirmed by Tariq Aziz in February
1983 (37) and probably concerned about 200,000 b/d of
Saudi Arabian Light and 50,000 b/d of Khafji and Hout
crude (Neutral Zone) for the first quarter; this was
probably raised to 200,000 b/d of Arabian Light
(henceforth AL) and 130,000 b/d of Neutral Zone
(henceforth NZ) crude for the second. From July onwards
more deals became known, with Japanese companies
(**Mitsubishi, Marubeni, Sumitomo**) lifting most of the NZ
crude under an arrangement between Iraq and the Saudi and
Kuwaiti governments, and involving the **Arabian National**

Oil Company (who has the main NZ concession and is jointly owned by those two governments and Japan). But these counterpart oil sales also served as payments to Sri Lanka, India, South Korea and the Philippines. 50/50 production arrangements for NZ crude under this scheme (between Saudi Arabia and Kuwait) were reported from July 1983; according to the **Wall Street Journal**, however, it was only at the end of September that Saudi Arabia started giving 130,000 b/d of NZ crude and 70,000 b/d of Arabian Light, in stead of all the latter quality (38).

Counterpart oil sales, therefore, appear to have followed the pattern laid out below:

1983	1st q.:	Saudi Arabia	200,000 b/d	(AL)
		Kuwait	50,000 b/d	(NZ)
	2nd q.:	Saudi Arabia	200,000 b/d	(AL)
		Kuwait	50,000 b/d	(NZ)
	3rd q.:	Saudi Arabia	200,000 b/d	(AL, + NZ?)
		Kuwait	130,000 b/d	(NZ)
	4th q.:	Saudi Arabia	200,000 b/d	(70,000 NZ; 130,000 AL)
		Kuwait	130,000 b/d	(NZ)
1984		Saudi Arabia	200,000 b/d	
		Kuwait	130,000 b/d	
1985		Saudi Arabia	200,000 b/d	
		Kuwait	130,000 b/d	

As indicated, the counterpart oil sales continued throughout 1984 and 1985. The agreement was scheduled to end at the beginning of 1986, and in principle, Iraq must pay back these loans in oil as soon as the war situation allows. Although the Iraqis stated officially that they were seeking an extension of the agreement for another year (39), Saudi press and other sources in late 1985 still indicated that would be unlikely (40), since Iraq's own exports had been boosted by upto 500,000 b/d via the Saudi East-West Line (see section C). It looked probable, therefore, that counterpart sales would be cut substantially. The new situation obtaining in the latest phase of the conflict (from February 1986), however, induced both Kuwait and Saudi Arabia to accede to Iraq's request. It appears, however, that the amount of crude allocated to Iraq has been reduced from 330,000 b/d to 310,000 b/d., divided between 125,000 b/d of Khafji crude from both, and another 60,000 b/d in Arabian Light from Saudi Arabia. Official confirmation of this agreement (officially between the **Iraqi National Oil Company** and the **Arabian Oil Company**) was given by Iraqi oil Minister

Ahmad Qasim Taqi in an interview with the Kuwaiti
newspaper **Al-Qabas** in May. Earlier reports that the
renewal would run for another three years, were neither
confirmed nor denied (41).

The first three years of oil swaps brought Iraq the
equivalent of about $ 6.1 billion from Saudi Arabia and $
3.6 billion from Kuwait, or a total of approximately $
9.7 billion (taking into account the varying oil prices
and assuming the Saudi contribution to have consisted of
Arabian Light up to the end of September 1983). Given
that production costs have to be subtracted, and that the
official sales prices have usually been some 93 % of
posted prices, the amount Iraq in fact received was
probably closer to $ 9 bn. Together with the financial
aid arrived at above, this means Arab Gulf aid by the end
of 1985 amounted to the equivalent of about $ 40 bn.

B. General Economic Agreements

Agreements covering several aspects of economic
co-operation, usually trade, industrial co-ordination,
transport, exchange of training and expertise (e.g in
agriculture, were concluded between Iraq and Qatar
(1980)(42), Bahrain (1982)(43), and Saudi Arabia
(1984)(44). Following up on these and earlier
agreements, joint committees were set up, and cooperation
protocols signed, between Iraq and all the Arab Gulf
states. These committees have been meeting regularly
(45).

C. Oil and Oil Policies

The trend towards an Iraqi oil policy more in alignment
with that of the other Arab Gulf states became
increasingly evident in 1981. Thus, after consultation
with Kuwait and Qatar, prices were jointly raised by $ 4
a barrel to $ 36 a barrel (as agreed in Bali), with
effect from 1 January 1981 (46). This rise
notwithstanding, Iraq in the course of that year actually
joined forces with Saudi Arabia against the 'radicals' in
trying to keep oil prices down (47). Some irritation with
Saudi over-production remained initially, in keeping with
Iraq's traditional ideological posture, but the incident
in August-September 1981, when critical remarks by oil
Minister Abdulkarim were quickly denied ever to have been
made, showed that such feelings had by then lost all
practical relevance. It was at this time that the first
talks were held about an Iraqi pipeline through the

Kingdom (see below), which helps explain the changing parameters of oil policy. Oil Minister Abdulkarim was replaced by Qasim Ahmad Taqi in July 1982 (48). When it became clear that Iraq would acquire a greater export capacity again, the Iraqi government did press the other Arab Gulf governments to support it in its demand for a higher OPEC quota (which stood at 1.2 million b/d - see Chapters III to VI). That demand was not initially connected with an explicit threat to act unilaterally. This changed in July 1985, when Deputy Oil Minister Al-Chalabi stated that Iraq wanted to maintain OPEC's unity and hoped for an arrangement before the end of September (when the extra capacity via the Saudi East-West line became available), but that it would "go ahead and ship, with OPEC permission or not" (49). Tariq Aziz confirmed in late September that Iraq was asking for a 1.7 million b/d quota (50). Saudi Arabia and Kuwait appeared willing to support some rise in Iraq's quota, but in the outcome of the October 1985 OPEC conference in Vienna, the conflicting demands of pushing up individual production and of maintaining oil prices, left no space for an accommodation of Iraq's wishes. Iraq subsequently unilaterally raised its own quota to 1.7 mbd (51).

The other Gulf producers ,too, however, had stepped up their efforts to at least maintain or, in the case of Saudi Arabia, recapture their market share. Netback deals (linking the price of the crude to the price which the buyers can obtain when putting their refined products on the market) became in vogue mainly from December 1985 and increasingly since. It was the Saudi switch to such special arrangements - starting with their decision to sell crude on special terms to some big US buyers in the summer of 1985 - which provided a major spark to the escalating price war. Iraq too, struggled for its share with discounts; ironically, after the Japanese (reacting against the Saudi-American deal) lowered their liftings of Saudi crude, Iraq immediately stepped in and offered special rates to the Japanese, for Iraqi oil which was to be lifted from Yanbu and was made available through the Saudi East-West Line (52). That there should be rumours about friction between the two allies, is understandable in these circumstances. But their common interests were far more important; and in the emerging split in OPEC one could observe that Iraqi and Arab Gulf oil policies were growing ever closer. Iraq in 1986 clearly belonged to that group within OPEC (with the Arab Gulf producers) which had opted for a market share confrontation with non-OPEC producers, by pushing up production and keeping prices low for the time being (Saudi Arabia and Kuwait also suggested a rise in Iraq's quota to 1.8 mbd, after

the Iraqis had stated their demand for a minimum of over
2 mbd - a suggestion which was predictably rejected
(53)). Iran has reacted furiously to this policy,
accusing Saudi Arabia and Kuwait of "collusion with the
enemies of Islam" and warning that, if this were proved,
action would be taken (54). Indeed, Prime Minister
Mussavi explicitly linked the war and particularly the
February offensives with the "oil conspiracy"; he
indicated that Iran wished to bring down the volume of
oil produced, if necessary by means of attacks on Iraqi
oil fields (55). Iran feels that bringing down the oil
prices was a deliberate plot on the part of the Arab Gulf
states to hit Iran. This seems unlikely, considering the
financial difficulties which low prices have afflicted
upon Iraq and the Arab Gulf. But the triple sabotage
carried out in mid-June against Kuwait's oil
installations, has been linked to Kuwaiti oil policy
(although Iran accused Iraq of being responsible).
Kuwait's Oil Minister Sheikh Ali Khalifa Al-Sabah
suggested a similar interpretation when insisting, after
the blasts, that the Emirate's policy would not change
(56).

The idea of a pipeline via the Gulf states

The idea of a pipeline connecting Iraq and the GCC states
was already under consideration in early 1981 (57). In
July of that year, Iraq announced plans for an oil link
across Kuwait and Saudi Arabia (58), and in September
Yamani declared that Saudi Arabia supported the idea of a
pipeline across the Kingdom, on condition that Iraq
financed the project and built its own terminal (59). The
Kuwaiti involvement was dropped in mid-1982 (60),
however, and plans for the link across Saudi Arabia were
delayed for some time due to Saudi reluctance to carry
the costs (61). In the spring of 1983 Iraq confirmed that
the principles of an Iraqi oil outlet through Saudi
Arabia were agreed upon, leaving only technicalities to
be settled: a pipeline to Yanbu would be built, utilising
finance provided by several Western companies (62). In
October the wider Iraq-GCC link received attention again.
Iraq declared that it wished to participate, and was
included in the feasibility studies (63). This project
subsequently dropped out of sight again, however, only to
re-emerge in 1985. The first clear Saudi statement (later
confirmed by Iraq) providing information about what the
preliminary project agreement concerning an Iraqi-Saudi
link entailed, came in November 1983: a first stage
would involve the construction of a 500,000 b/d spur
from southern Iraq to the East-West Line, and a second
the extension of the Iraqi line parallel to the Saudi

pipeline. Financing was declared to be "entirely up to Iraq" (64).

The design contract was awarded in March 1984. Later that year Saudi Arabia agreed not to charge transit fees, although Iraq would still have to compensate landowners along the route (65). Work on the first stage (IPSA-1) started in the autumn, and was completed in July 1985 (66). Iraq did receive Arab Gulf support in that APICORP raised about half of the cost of that stage as two loans for a total of $ 255 million (67). Iraqi oil began being transported via the new outlet from September 1985. Iraqi Oil Minister Ahmad Qasim Taqi officially announced the opening on 30 September (68). Japan appears to have been the main taker of Iraqi oil delivered at Yanbu.

In December 1985, the Saudi Council of Ministers approved the route and the new terminal for the second stage (IPSA-2) (69). The different sections of the project were tendered in May and June 1986, and **Aramco** was given the responsibility of overseeing the project for the Iraqis. Completion is foreseen for mid-1988, with cost estimates ranging upto $ 1.5 bn. Together with the expansion of the capacity of the East-West line and IPSA-1, IPSA-2 will increase Iraq's export capacity via the Kingdom to 1.6 mbd (Iraq's producton mid-1986 was close to 2 mbd)(70).

Finally, the concept of a strategic pipeline of GCC producers, which would also link up with Iraq, was again discussed at a meeting of the GCC Oil Ministers in Riyadh in October 1985. The project, which would avoid the Gulf as an export channel, would involve a 1,700 kms long pipeline, and cost $ 2-3 bn, according to a feasibility study by Dhahran's University of Petroleum and Minerals (71).

D. Joint projects: industrial and agricultural cooperation

Most projects and cooperation of this kind were multilateral, within the framework of Arab and Gulf institutions. Iraq continued and further activated its membership in ventures and organisations formed before the war - confirming SAKR's expectations (72) - although financial constraints from 1983 forced some cutbacks in participation. The country remained an active member in such organisations as the Conference of Ministers of Agriculture of the Gulf States and the Arabian Peninsula (CMAGSAP, based in Riyadh); the **Arab Maritime Petroleum**

Transport Co (AMPTC, Kuwait); the **United Arab Shipping Co** (UASC, Kuwait); **Gulf International Bank** (GIB, Manama); the **Arab Petroleum Investment Corporation** (APICORP, Dhahran); the **Arab Company for Industrial Investment** (ACII, Baghdad) which was only joined by Qatar in December 1981 (other members are Libya, Jordan, YAR, Tunisia, Morocco)(73) ; and the **Gulf Organisation for Industrial Consulting** (GOIC, Doha)(see Appendix VI).

Iraq's April 1981 statement that it would "definitely take part" in all GOIC-sponsored ventures, was followed up by the Iraqi government taking a 20 % stake in GARMCO, the **Gulf Aluminium Rolling Company** (74). GOIC also suggested setting up a sheet glass factory in Iraq. This was supported by Qatar, Saudi Arabia and Bahrain, in addition to Iraq itself which promised to grant tax concessions and other privileges (75). With APICORP, Iraq agreed in September 1980 to set up an **Arab Company for Chemical Detergents** (ACCD or **Aradet**); Iraq and APICORP both took a 25 % share, the rest being offered to OAPEC members. The agreement was signed in March 1981; it was decided to set up two plants in Iraq: one in Baiji and one in Al-Qaim (76). Saudi Arabia joined in late 1982 (77). The idea of establishing a new **Arab Organisation for Industrialisation** (to replace the one which had been defunct since Egypt was ostracised) was also pursued (78), and the GCC proposed the inclusion of Iraq in a convertible oil-water Gulf pipeline. Another example of cooperation was the June 1982 meeting of representatives of chemical fertiliser companies from Kuwait, Saudi Arabia, Qatar and Iraq in Doha for technical talks involving the running and maintenance of production plants (79).

From 1983 the impact of the war made itself felt. The sheet glass project was postponed due to financial difficulties stemming from the war (80), and Iraqi investors were reported to have withdrawn from a GOIC-sponsored glass fibre venture set up in Saudi Arabia, because of currency problems (81). A considerable amount of cooperation and joint investment nevertheless went ahead. Plans for an antibiotics factory under the wings of the **Arab Company for Drug Industries and Medical Appliances** (ACDIMA, Amman) were further pursued (82). **Aradet** was officially incorporated in Baghdad in December 1983; Iraq and APICORP both raised their stake to 32 % and the rest was taken up by Saudi Arabia, Kuwait, the **Arab Mining Co** (Amman) and **The Arab Investment Co** (TAIC, Riyadh) (83). The project for the two plants reached the bidding stage by April 1983, with completion expected for 1987 (84). A $ 35-40 million aluminium foil mill was

planned for Bahrain, with participation of Iraq and the
GCC states (except for the UAE) (85), and in the
framework of ACII a $ 1 billion seamless steel pipes
factory was to be built in Nasiriya. Finally, it was
announced in February 1985 that the GOIC would finalise
plans for the postponed glass works in Iraq (85). Late
December, the agreement to set up the joint company was
signed by the Iraqis and the GOIC; feasibility studies
are to be updated. Bahrain seems to have dropped out of
the scheme, but the Arab Mining Co. will now also
participate (86).

The Gas Link with Kuwait

A dramatic illustration of the growing economic links
between Kuwait and Iraq is provided by the scheme,
initiated in 1985, to pipe gas from the Rumaila oil
fields in southern Iraq, to Kuwait. The latter country,
having no non-associated gas reserves of its own, has
been experiencing severe gas shortages due to falling oil
production. This has meant it has had to use more liquid
fuels in meeting the energy needs of its industry, a
process both more expensive and more polluting (87).
Preliminary talks with Iraq took place in July 1985;
responsibility was in the hands of **Kuwait Petroleum Corp.**
(KPC). Iraq's National Assembly endorsed the draft
agreement on providing Kuwait with natural gas on 9
November 1985 and the official agreement was signed on
the 28th of that month (88). The scheme provides for
the construction of two pipelines, with a capacity of
respectively 400 million cubic feet a day of natural gas,
and some 40,000 barrels a day of condensates. KOC having
taken over executive responsibility for the project
from its parent KPC, another KPC subsidiary: **Braun & Co**
(part of the now wholly Kuwaiti-owned **Santa Fe Corp.**),
was chosen as project manager. In a first phase, from
June 1986, some 200 million cfd were scheduled to be
piped to Kuwait; this volume was due to double by the end
of October, reaching the full capacity of 400 mn cfd of
gas and 40,000 b/d of condensates. The deal should bring
at least an extra $ 500 million a year into Iraq's
coffers (89).

Agriculture

For an indication of the importance Iraq attaches to
agriculture and agricultural cooperation with the Gulf
states, reference may be made to SAKR (90). Iraq's
gradual movement towards **infitah,** also entailed providing
facilities for private Arab investment in agriculture.

Two main fields of cooperation can be discerned: the elusive plans for the provision of water to Kuwait and the Gulf; and multilateral, large-scale project cooperation with the Gulf.

In February 1981 Mana' al-Otaiba, the UAE Oil Minister, revealed information about a plan to build a convertible water-oil pipeline from Iraq to the Gulf. Nothing ever came of this, however. The more limited objective of a pipeline to bring water from Iraq to Kuwait, 'revived' before the war, seemed to make progress when, in early 1982, consultants were invited to submit designs for (a) a pipeline to carry 100 - 300 million gallons/day from Qasara (north of Basra) ; (b) a pipeline to take water from the Shatt al-Arab. The Iraqi Irrigation Minister stated in March of that year that Iraq had "agreed to provide Kuwait and Jordan with water, and (that it was) also prepared to give water to the Gulf states" (91). In that same month, however, the project was shelved, and for the next three years there was no evidence of any follow-up. This probably stemmed from Kuwait's refusal to let any part of Bubiyan or Warba to Iraq. It was not until mid-1985 that the scheme received official attention again. In June 1985, a Kuwaiti team went to Baghdad to discuss technical details of the project and Kuwait's Minister of Electricity and Water confirmed in September that his country would eventually take water from southern Iraq - though not until at least four years after the end of the Gulf War (92). It is not clear whether or not that qualification still stands at the time of writing: in 1986 Kuwait set up a committee to study the project; the US' **Braun Transworld Corp.** - Kuwaiti-owned and already involved in the gas-line scheme - was given the task of collecting preliminary data on the basis of which a feasibility study was to be done by an international consultant. The project would supply up to 350 million gallons of water a day, of which 200 million would be for drinking (93).

Iraq continued playing an active role in CMAGSAP. Two projects which originated in 1979 were implemented during the war: a $ 70 mn scheme to develop 20,000 hectares of irrigated land in central Iraq; and a $ 30 mn project to produce 83,000 tons of certified seeds per year from six centres in Iraq, Saudi Arabia and North Yemen. These were to draw 32 % of their finance from the host country, another 32 % from the Gulf Authority for Food and Agriculture, 16 % from private investors and 20 % from commercial loans (94). The 6th CMAGSAP meeting in 1981 proposed a scheme which was eventually incorporated in an agreement signed in Baghdad in March 1983, between the

Iraqi Agriculture and Land Reclamation Minister and the
Director-General of the Arab Organisation for
Agricultural Development. According to this agreement a
joint Gulf project was to be set up to grow cereal,
fodder and vegetables on an area of approximately 60,000
acres in Iraq; funding would come from the Arab Fund for
Agricultural Development (95). A fourth project involving
Iraqi-Gulf cooperation in the agricultural sector emerged
from talks which the Iraqi government held in 1983 with
Kuwait's **Oriental Import Co.** A $ 100 mn scheme to
produce farm products in Iraq for export to the Gulf was
envisaged. The project, for which **Oriental** did a
pre-feasibility study, would involve 300,000 hectares;
TAIC was reported to be interested in providing finance
(96). This latter initiative fitted into the Iraqi
government's policy in recent years, of liberalising
regulations on agricultural investment, as documented by
SPRINGBORG (97).

On a bilateral level, technical advice was given to the
UAE in land reclamation and irrigation (98), and
agricultural cooperation was an important part of the
general economic agreement with Bahrain; in 1984 an
offer to Bahrain was made to provide palm saplings and
agricultural training (99).

E. Trade, Business and Financing

1. Agreements and orientation

As indicated above, the general economic agreements
concluded between Iraq and the Gulf states contained
important provisions on trade cooperation. Iraq's
infitah, which had started before the war, unfolded
further (see SAKR, 1982 and SPRINGBORG, 1985). Ample
facilities were provided for Arab (effectively Gulf)
investors; particularly Kuwaitis took great advantage of
this.

Early in 1981 the Iraqi deputy Trade Minister met with
some Kuwaiti businessmen, while on a visit to Kuwait, and
stated that the emirate was "considered an extension of
the Iraqi market" (100). This conception seems to have
been fundamental to Iraqi government attitudes. At the
3rd meeting of the joint Iraqi-Kuwaiti economic committee
in November 1983, discussions were held on customs
tariffs, ways of increasing trade, and the facilitating
of Kuwaiti customs procedures for Iraqi imports
transiting through Kuwait. The possibility of Iraqi

purchases of Kuwaiti manufactured goods on credit terms
was also raised (101). It is not clear whether any
tangible results were achieved.

Between Iraq and Bahrain a free trade agreement already
existed for aluminium and agricultural goods. Trade
cooperation was a concern of the economic agreement of
1982, and the joint economic committee meetings between
the two countries discussed ways to ensure a better
implementation of the pact. One outcome of this was the
setting up by each country of a trade centre in the other
(102).

Again, in the Iraqi-Qatari economic agreement trade
formed a major part. The joint economic committee
meetings called for increased trade and, in 1985, more
goods were exempted from customs duty (103). Iraq and
Oman signed a trade agreement in May 1983 (104).

It is useful to note some of the provisions of the
Saudi-Iraqi economic and trade agreement of 1984, since
this reflects particular Iraqi concerns. The agreement
stipulates free trade in certain products, mainly
industrial, animal, and agricultural produce, and natural
resources; makes arrangements to stimulate and facilitate
transit trade; and envisages full customs coordination.
Capital invested by either country or their citizens is
guaranteed against expropriation; joint economic and
development projects, by private investors as well as by
the government are promoted; investments in each other's
country are given the same privileges as national
projects and businesses. A joint economic committee was,
in addition, set up (104).

Iraq, therefore, now has similar agreements with each of
the Six. On a multilateral level, Iraq was kept out of
the GCC market arrangement, but the Iraqi Chamber of
Commerce is a member of the Association of Gulf Chambers
of Commerce, Industry and Agriculture.

2. Cross-border private capital involvement in industry, contracting, agriculture and services

The involvement of Iraq in Arab joint ventures as a
partner not only of governments but also of
non-government bodies, has been mentioned above. So also
has the country's economic liberalisation allowing for
instance a 20 % participation of private capital in
agricultural projects (105). The interest and increasing
involvement of Gulf companies in Iraq was reflected in

the partipation in a November 1980 conference on "Iraq: business strategies for the 1980s" where out of 90 represented companies, 11 were from the Gulf (106). The trend, noted by SAKR (107), for many Kuwaiti companies to open offices in Baghdad continued and increased in 1981.

In 1981 at least 10 major contracts (in construction, sewerage, etc.) were awarded to Kuwaiti firms by Iraqi state organisations. The biggest one was a $ 210 million contract between the Ministry of Defence and **Fiafi Trading and Contracting Co**, for work from 1981 into 1983. The management of another Kuwaiti-based company successful on the Iraqi market could claim, in mid-1981, that there had been no slow-down in business since the start of the war. In 1982, however, only one major contract appears to have been awarded to a Kuwaiti company, although smaller contracts continued to be signed (108).

From 1982, payments delays for Kuwaiti companies began to occur. Some of these, as in the big **Keir** and **Musaad al-Saleh** case against the Iraqi government in 1983, led to withdrawal from contracts. In many cases banks in the GCC rejected requests from Arab contractors for foreign exchange loans for work in Iraq, despite guarantees from the Rafidain Bank and the Iraqi Central Bank. Some Kuwaiti companies were given assistance by the Kuwait government, but Iraq's foreign exchange restrictions caused problems for many (109). From 1983 onwards, business, already at a lower level, tended to shift to transport. Thus, a Kuwaiti company in June 1983 gained a contract with the Iraqi State Organisation for the Distribution of Oil and Gas Products, for the transport of "several thousand tonnes a day" of oil products from Baiji to Aqaba (110), and in early 1986 another Kuwaiti firm landed a contract to transport 20,000 tonnes of urea fertiliser to Iraq (111). But Kuwaiti private interests have still scored some successes in other fields on the Iraqi market. **Al-Rowdah Trading & Contracting Co.**, for instance, has been doing considerable work for the Baghdad Sewerage Board since 1980, and in mid-1986 looked set to win another contract on an extension of the Iraqi capital's sewerage system (112). The design competition for a $ 60 mn presidential guest palace in Mosul, started in 1984, was won in January 1986 by the only non-Iraqi architect to be invited, Kuwait's **Archicentre** (113).

The only other Gulf state with important involvement in Iraqi contracts, was Dubai. The contract for the Mosul Hotel went to a Dubai contractor in 1981; and another was, until 1984, completing work on large contracts begun in 1979 and 1980 (114). In February 1986 a Saudi construction company (**Manufacturing & Building Co.**, of Riyadh) was reported to have initiated preliminary partnership agreements for work in Iraq (115). Prior to that, Saudi commercial activity in Iraq was limited mainly to truck transport.

As for Iraqi involvement in the Gulf states, the evidence is scanty (116). The way appears to be open for the development of private Iraqi investment in those states, thanks to the above mentioned agreements. But there is no evidence of major Iraqi contracts in any of the Six since 1981.

3. Trade flows

Statistical data on trade are provided in Appendix IV. All comments made below are based on these, unless otherwise stated.

Iraq-Kuwait. The level of Iraqi exports to Kuwait before the war had dropped to around $6 - 7 mn per year, and the war did not change this. In 1982 the value of Iraqi exports to Kuwait doubled - also in proportion to Iraq's total exports (In Kuwait's total imports, the Iraqi share jumped from 0.09 % in 1981 to 0.13 in 1982). The doubling may be explained by transit of Iraqi phosphates, but the amount remained in any case rather insignificant, and dropped again in 1983. From mid-1986, however, the revenues from gas exports to Kuwait will change the picture completely, raising the total figure for Iraq's exports to Kuwait to over $ 500 mn a year from 1987.

Kuwaiti exports to Iraq began to rise sharply after 1978, roughly doubling every year up to and including 1981. In absolute terms, therefore, the rise in 1981 was the biggest, amounting to half a billion dollars. But from 1982 onwards the level of these exports started to decline again, to under $ 0.8 bn in 1983, mainly because no more cement was sold (117). The war thus had two contradictory effects. In 1981 and 1982, the political decision by the Iraqi government to boost consumption, the development of infrastructure, and economic activity in general (thus shielding the population psychologically and economically from the war), in conjunction with the fact that the war situation had made Kuwait a vital transshipment port for Iraqi goods, caused the rise in Iraqi imports from and via Kuwait to be kept up exponentially (In mid-1981 sales of Kuwaiti merchants were up by 20 % over the previous year mainly because of

Iraqi demand (118)). But in the later period, from 1983 onwards, many of the projects started earlier had been completed, and the financial squeeze was making itself felt. The Iraqi economy thus had less needs for imports (e.g. cement) and less purchasing power. The flow of goods decreased considerably, as did Iraq's % share in Kuwait's exports. But, although discrepancies in available figures make interpretation dificult, it appears that that share was maintained at a level above the one prevalent before the war.

Iraq-Saudi Arabia. Iraqi exports to Saudi Arabia prior to 1984 remained insignificant: an increase in 1983 still left them at a somewhat lower level than the $ 6 mn peak of 1979. In 1984, however, according to **MEED** figures, Iraqi exports to the Kingdom quintupled to $ 25 mn. Saudi exports to Iraq were more important, and showed an even more striking rise: from about $ 2mn in 1978 to over $ 50 mn in 1982. Even as a proportion of total Saudi exports, the rise in Iraq's share was 7-fold. Clearly, however, this rise had set in before the war (reaching c. $ 20 mn in 1980). Not surprisingly, in 1983 the value of exports to Iraq dropped again to below its 1981-level (c. $ 43 mn f.o.b.). Iraqi war-imposed austerity thus clearly had its impact, but the main body of expanded exports was left intact.The effect of the 1984 agreement was still awaited at the time of writing.

Iraq - Bahrain (119). Iraqi exports to Bahrain were small. They peaked in 1978 at c. $ 6mn, but that was a 'freak' year. By 1980 they dropped to less than 1/5 of the 1978 figure; they have dropped even further since. No significant conclusion about the impact of the war can be drawn. There was a considerable rise in the volume of Bahraini exports to Iraq from 1980 (c. $ 21 mn) through to 1982 (c. $ 47 mn), followed by a sharp drop in 1983 to about 15 % of the 1982 figure. The rise seems to have been due to increased Iraqi imports of consumer goods via Bahrain, and of aluminium from ALBA for the construction boom, both of which were indirectly caused by the war. Financial hardship from 1983 may explain the sharp drop which occurred at that time (120).

Iraq - UAE. Iraqi exports to the UAE in 1980 fell to a low of c. $ 1 mn (0.01 % of the UAE's imports). This was followed by an increase to c. $ 8 mn by 1983, which represents a real as well as a proportionate increase over the previous high in 1976. The amount of this trade, however, is too small to allow firm conclusions. UAE exports to Iraq, following the mold of the trade relationships with the other Gulf states treated above,

were more important. They climbed steadily from virtually
nothing in the   early 1970s to around $ 80 mn in 1981 and
1982. This also represents   a   significant   proportionate
rise. Non-oil   exports   to Iraq as a percentage of total
non-oil exports rose from 0.8 % in   1978 to 5.28 % in
1982. The rise had started in 1978 and 1979, so it is
hard to point out the impact of the war. The further
doubling which occurred in 1981, however, may partly
have been a consequence of increased transit trade, so an
argument similar to that for the cases of Bahrain and, on
a   different   scale,   Kuwait   may   be   followed.   The
1983-figures indicate that the parallel continued, with
UAE-to-Iraq trade dropping again to between the 1980 and
1981 levels.

Trade in both directions with Qatar and Oman was too
small for their evolution to be a significant topic
for comment. The economic and trade agreements concluded
must   have   had   as   much, if not more, a political
background than an economic one. Mention must be made,
nevertheless, of the exceptional Qatari steel exports to
Iraq in 1980, bringing total Iraqi imports from that
country to around $ 25 mn for that year.

4. Finance

The Iraqi financial needs created by the cost of the war
effort and the two-year imports boom, were, as has
already been indicated, partly covered by commercial
loans (or what were considered as such), and aid via
normal channels such as the Arab Monetary Fund (AMF) or
the Islamic Development Bank (IDB). The former could
consist either of payments to Iraq, or of financing for
companies working in or supplying Iraq. A considerable
role in this was played by Arab Gulf capital and
institutions. The loans extended in this manner are
listed below.

1981   (a) 4 Kuwaiti Banks co-managed two loans,
totalling the equivalent of c. $ 32 mn, for financing
Iraqi contracts of the Kuwaiti **International Contracting
Group** (121). (b) **Gulf International Bank** (GIB) was
mandated by Hyundai to arrange a $ 20 mn loan and a $ 60
mn revolving facility for letters of credit. The five
banks involved were all Arab and Gulf-based (122). (c) **Al
Bahrain Arab African Bank** led a syndicate of all-Arab
banks for a $ 20 mn loan to a Philippino company working
in Iraq (123).

1982   Five Kuwaiti banks were behind some $ 23.5 mn in medium-term loans and guarantee facilities to finance participation of an Italian-Swiss group (**Technipetrol**) in the contract for the Baiji refinery (124).

1983   (a) The **Rafidain Bank's** $ 500 mn Euroloan, which had been organised in 1982, was signed in the spring of 1983. It was lead-managed by **Alubaf Arab International Bank**, owned by UBAF's all-Arab holding company UBAC. Of the 10 lead-managers (for $ 50 mn each), 6 represented Gulf capital; the same was true for 4 out of the 5 co-lead managers ($ 20 mn each), 2 out of the 3 managers at the $ 5 - $ 10 mn level, and 5 out of the 11 smaller contributors (125). (b) A $ 120 mn loan to INOC was arranged by the **Arab Banking Corporation** (ABC) and **APICORP** to finance the expansion of the Kirkuk-Dortyol pipeline. Of the other contributors, 7 were Gulf-based banks with Gulf capital (126). (c) An **AMF** loan of $ 85 mn was obtained as balance of payments support (127). (d) The **IDB** lent $ 25 mn to support the import of semi-finished and industrial goods , and (e) two more unspecified loans came from the **Arab Fund for Economic and Social Development** (AFESD) and the **AMF** (128). This brought total assistance from Arab regional and national development institutions (i.e. exclusive of the **AMF**) to $ 84.5 mn for the year - the first time anything was forthcoming from those sources (129).

1984   (a) The **IDB** provided two $ 20 mn loans, for palm oil imports from Malaysia (130). Further support from **AFESD** and the **Kuwait Fund for Arab Economic Development** (KFAED) brought total assistance from Arab development institutions in 1984 to $ 81 mn (131). (b) **APICORP** raised two loans for a total of $ 205 mn, to help finance the Iraqi spur to the East-West Line (132).

1985   (a) **IDB** loans amounted to at least some $ 40 mn (133). (b) An **AMF** loan of $ 91 mn, signed on 25 December, brought total **AMF** lending to Iraq to $ 270.9 mn (134). (c) A new $ 500 mn Euroloan, led by **GIB**, took a long time to negotiate; the signing was finally announced on 25 October. **GIB** itself put up $ 124 mn, and the other eight Arab participating banks brought the share of Arab (effectively Gulf) capital to $ 314 mn out of the total. The return was thought to be only 1 % over a year (135). Since on a normal L/C arrangement with Rafidain the return is about 5 % over 6 months, , this indicates that the loan implies strong political support for Iraq. This confirms the impression acquired earlier, that as far as the Arab banking world and aid institutions go, 'commercial' and 'development' loans have been a discreet way of providing aid, and were often prompted by the governments concerned.

1986   The **IDB** from January   to early June had given Iraq
another 7 loans for a total   of $ 77 mn, for palm oil,
jute   and   fertiliser imports, and copper rods from Saudi
Arabia (136).

F. Transport and Communication

Stipulations about transport links figured in some of the
general economic agreements concluded, specifically those
with Kuwait and Saudi Arabia.   The role of Kuwait was, of
course, particularly important in this field. Even before
the war Kuwait had become an important   transshipment
port, making available 4 berths for Iraq-bound cargo (See
Ch. I, C). One of the reasons for the visit of the Iraqi
Deputy Trade Minister to Kuwait in January 1981, was to
talk about expanding these facilities in Kuwaiti ports
(137). Following the visit, 3 more berths in Shuaiba were
set   aside for Iraq-bound cargo. Road transport from
Kuwait approximately tripled in 1981 (see section E.3);
some local Kuwaiti transport companies were at that time
buying fleets simply for Iraqi goods (138). But in 1982,
as indicated above, the cost of the war began to bring
spending and thus imports down, causing difficulties for
those truckers who had over-extended themselves (139).
Still, the volume of Iraq-bound transport was greater
than before the war, and convoys of Kuwaiti trucks
crossing   into   Iraq   remained a prominent part of
Kuwaiti-Iraqi traffic. This provides some indication of
the Kuwaiti will to support Iraq, for Rafsanjani had
threatened in 1982 that Iran would take action "if the
caravan of trucks to Iraq continues" (140).

In November 1983, an agreement was concluded to
facilitate Kuwaiti customs procedures for Iraqi trade
passing through Kuwait (see E.1). Even though overall
Iraqi imports dropped, the war created specific needs.
Thus falling rice production in the Basra area, partly
due to flooding of some marshes to keep out the Iranians,
meant a big increase in rice imports: these seem to have
reached about 600,000 tonnes, all delivered at Shuaiba
and forwarded by truck to Iraq (141).

In another area of cooperation, an agreement was
concluded in 1984, between the Iraqi State Organisation
for Civil Aviation and Kuwait Airways. This envisaged the
coordination of interests in flights, airfreight, landing
rights, and cooperation in supply, training, employment,
automatic   reservation,   and maintenance.   (142).   As

regards   air links: at the time of writing (summer 1986),
six flights a week connected Baghdad with Kuwait (there
were no flights between Kuwait and Iran).

The UAE also served as   a   transshipment point for
Iraq-bound goods, but this did   not   indicate a political
stand. Indeed, a major part of the distressed cargo which
was   accepted   in UAE ports was destined   for   Iran.   Air
connections between the UAE and Iran increased during the
first half of   the   1980s: in   mid-1986 there   were   17
flights   a   week   (of which 15 from/to Dubai), as against
no direct flights to/from Baghdad. This provides another
illustration of particularly Dubai's economic orientation
towards Iran rather than Iraq.   Direct   dialling   between
Iraq   and   the   UAE, however, which had stopped since the
outbreak of the war, was resumed in June 1982 (143).

The Saudi role in passing   on Iraqi imports (arms, steel,
etc.) has been highlighted earlier (some   15 % of Dammam
port's   capacity,   for instance, was handling Iraqi goods
by October 1982) (145).   In   November   1983 **Saudia**
introduced a weekly   flight   between Baghdad and   Jeddah,
via Riyadh (146). At the   time of writing, four flights a
week   connected Baghdad with the Kingdom   (which   had   no
permanent air links with Iran).

Oman   and   Iraq   in   March   1985   signed   an   agreement
(initially   arrived   at   in   December   1983)   covering
cooperation   in   airline services (passenger   and   cargo)
and airports (147).   By   mid-1986 there were, however, no
direct   flights   between   Muscat and Baghdad   (nor   any
Iranian airport). One weekly flight was operating between
Baghdad and Bahrain (which   had   no   direct connection to
Iran), but none between Baghdad and Doha - easily reached
from   Bahrain   (Doha   did at this time   have   one   weekly
connection with Shiraz).

Finally, the project for a Gulf   rail   merits mention. A
specific agreement was first reached with Kuwait in April
1981: both countries were to be responsible for   the part
of the link on their territory; it was to be a dual track
to   enable   passenger   trains to travel at speeds of upto
250 km an hour.   The   minimum   annual   cargo   volume   was
forecast to be some 5 million tons. The two countries put
out   a joint tender, and in the same year the project was
joined by,   first,   Saudi Arabia, Qatar, and the UAE, and
then also Oman. A   pre-feasibility study   (undertaken by
Transmark, a **British Rail** subsidiary) was completed in
November 1981 (148). Only   in   late   1983 was there again
evidence of some progress, when the GCC and Iraq
commissioned   a   detailed   feasibility   study   by

Transmark, for a 1700 km track. Reportedly, the **Gulf Investment Co** (GIC) would finance the project (149). The study should have been completed by mid-1984, but no further action was then taken, parallelling the delays in the water scheme. A major obstacle no doubt was the outstanding border issue between Iraq and Kuwait, in turn connected to the islands question. By 1986, a new factor had arisen in the shape of dwindling oil revenues: in January of that year, it was announced that the plans were shelved because of the cost involved (an estimated $ 4 bn); more research was said to be needed (150).

G. Socio-cultural Relations

In the field of education and science, Iraq maintained its pre-war involvement in several pan-Gulf institutions and activities. In addition, an OAPEC meeting held in Baghdad determined that an "Arab Oil Training Institute" would be established in Baghdad, to be 20 % Iraqi-funded. Further, a first Conference for Scientific Research in the Arab Gulf took place in Baghdad in May 1982, bringing together the heads of research centres in the Gulf (151). The Gulf University received the go-ahead from the seven Gulf Education Ministers in April 1981 (152). Iraq signed a cultural and scientific agreement with Qatar in August 1981 (153), and with Kuwait a cultural, scientific and information agreement was signed in May 1983, stipulating scientific cooperation particularly in the fields of petrochemicals, land reclamation and solar energy, and the exchange of scholarships (154).

Iraq, in addition to including the elements of information and media in these bilateral agreements, was also a very active member of all pan-Gulf institutions in this field, originating from the annual Conferences of Ministers of Information. Tangible results from the decisions of those conferences were the setting up of (a) the **Arab Gulf States Joint Programme Production Corporation** (Kuwait), which was to produce high-quality T.V. programmes (in the cultural, health, and children's fields, among others); (b) a Gulf TV corporation (**Gulf-vision**)(based in Saudi Arabia); (c) an **Information Documentation Centre** in Baghdad; (d) The **Gulf News Agency** (GNA)(based in Bahrain); and the **Popular Heritage Centre** in Qatar (155). There was coordination between Iraq and the Six in most aspects of information and media, and some further specialist functional organisations and institutes in the field were established (156).

Iraq took part in the annual Conferences of Gulf Ministers of Labour and Social Affairs, and hosted the 1984 Conference (157). On a bilateral level, a 3-year technical cooperation agreement was signed with the UAE in November 1983, involving the provision of expertise for training workers in the UAE, and the establishment of a joint committee. The agreement stipulated that Iraq would provide expertise on labour relations, wages, employment, industrial safety, care for the elderly and disabled, and juvenile delinquency; both sides agreed to organise activities in those fields (158). A further such agreement was signed in December 1985 (159).

In religious affairs, Iraq pulled closer to Saudi Arabia. The Saudi Pilgrimage and Awqaf Minister was received by Saddam Husein and his Iraqi counterpart in June 1984, for talks on cooperation (160). Saddam's attention to this aspect of relations had a clearly political motivation.

One indication of popular, rather than primarily governmental, Iraqi interaction with the Arab Gulf has been the interest shown in pan-Gulf socio-cultural events. Particularly the regular encounters in sporting events (only one of which is the annual Gulf Soccer Tournament) have received wide TV and media coverage and have been avidly followed by many Iraqis, as well as people in the GCC states.

Contrary to all the above, however, is the fact that it became somewhat more difficult for GCC nationals to visit Iraq. At the end of 1980, Iraq decided that from then on all Arab visitors would need entry visas. This rule included GCC citizens and was still in force at the time of writing (161). The decision was directly related to war-time security considerations.

NOTES TO CHAPTER VIII

1. See: **MEED**, 17-4-1981; 6-11-1981; 1-1-1982; **MEES**, 16-11-1981. Some confusion existed as to whether it was two loans ($ 4 bn) or three ($ 6 bn), but it is clear, contrary to what **MEED**, 1-1-1982, and **MEES**, 16-11-1981, say, that there was indeed a third loan, the draft bill for which was introduced in December, **after** the retroactive approval of the 1980 loan. This is explicitly confirmed by reports in the Kuwaiti press (**Al-Ra'y al-'Amm** and **Al-Siyasa**, 10-12-1981) and REUTERS (dispatch of 15-12-1981), all quoting parliamentary sources.

2. **Al-Ra'y al-'Amm**, 16-4-1981

3. AFP dispatch 20-4-1981; **MEED**, 16-11-1981

4. **MEED**, 12-11-1982

5. **Al-Nahar**, 25-5-1981

6. **MEES**, 16-11-1981

7. Compare **AER** 1983, p. 314; **FT**, 10-11-1982; **MEES**, 2-8-1982; **MEED**, 2-4-1982.

8. **MEED**, 4-3-1983.

9. **AER**, 1983, p. 314

10. **BW**, 6-12-1982; **EIU QER Iraq**, 1983,1, p. 11

11. Compare **MEES**, 2-8-1982; **MEED**, Iraq Special Report 1982 October, p. 4; **FT**, 10-11-1982; **MEED**, 12-11-1982; 19-11-1982.

12. **MEED**, 12-11-1982

13. See: ibid.; and 17-12-1982; **BW**, 6-12-1982.

14. **Agefi Review**, 5-2-1983; 12-2-1983; **MEER**, March 1983; confirmed in **AOG**, 16-2-1983.

15. **MEED**, 16-12-1983

16. See **MEES**, 2-8-1982

17. **EIU QER Iraq, Annual Supplement**, 1985, p. 15

18. QUANDT, 1984, p. 4

19. British industry sources; Gulf Banking sources; **EIU QER Iraq**, 1984,1, p.8

20. PE, June 1986

21. **FT**, 1-5-1986

22. See **MEED**, 29-3-1986

23. **FT**, 22-5-1986; PE June 1986 has a figure of $ 26.7 bn.

24. MUEHRING, 1984, p. 66

26. **MEED**, 29-3-1986

27. **MEED**, 17-5-1986

28. See **MEED**, 29-3-1986

29. ibid.

30. **MEES**, 26-5-1986

31. **MEES**, 2-6-1986

32. **MEED, Special Report. Kuwait,** April 1986, p.5

33. PE, January 1982, pp. 23-24

34. See also **MEED**, 25-9-1981; **FT**, 10-11-1981

35. PE, January 1982, p. 24

36. See **MEES**, 2-8-1982

37. **MEED**, 25-2-1982

38. See **AOG**, 16-6-1983;   1-8-1983;   16-8-1983;   **WSJ**, 24-10-1983; PE, August 1983, pp 311, 317; November 1984; **MEED**, 25-2-1983; **PIW**, 11-7-1983.

39. Tariq Aziz quoted in **WSJ**, 30-9-1985. See further **MEED**, 3-8-1985.

40. **MEED**, 9-11-1985

41. See **MEED**, 22-2-1986; 10-5-1986

42. **Al-Sharq al-Awsat,** 6-10-1980

43. SWB, ME/W , 5-10-1982

44. See the text of the agreement in **Alwaqai aliraqiya,** 20-3-1985.

45. **MEED,** 20-6-1984; 1-2-1985; **SWB,** ME/W 1340/A1/7, 28-5-1985; MW/W 11325/A1/5, 12-2-1985; ME/7864/A/11, 1-2-1985; **BO,** 28-10-1983; QNA dispatches of 19-5-1983 and 4-4-1984.

46. **MEES,** 12-1-1981

47. **Economist,** 25-7-1981

48. **PE,** August 1982, p. 340

49. **MEED,** 3-8-1985

50. **WSJ,** 30-9-1985

51. **SWB** ME/W 1360/i, 15-10-1985;   ME/W 1369/i, 17-12-1985.

52. **ST,** 22-9-1985

53. **MEES,** 24-3-1986

54. **MEES,** 17-2-1986; see also 10-2-1986.

55. **MEES,** 3-3-1986

56. **The Guardian,** 19-6-1986

57. **Observer,** 15-2-1981

58. **PE,** October 1981, p. 447

59. **MEED,** 25-9-1981; **MEES,** 12-7-1982

60. **MEES,** 12-7-1982

61. **MEED,** 3-12-1982; 25-2-1983

62. **MEED,** 25-2-1983; 4-3-1983

63. **PE,** November 1983, p. 432; **MEED,** 28-10-1983

64. OPECNA, 29-11-1983; **MEED,** 27-6-1984

65. **MEED,** 23-3-1984; 27-6-1984; 21-9-1984

66. MEED, 10-5-1985; **Middle East Newsletter. Saudi Arabia,** 8-7-1985

67. MEED, 2-11-1984

68. MEED, 5-10-1985

69. MEES, 10-2-1986

70. MEED, 10-5-1986; 7-6-1986

71. MEED, 19-10-1985

72. SAKR, 1982

73. For ACII see **MEED,** 11-2-1981; and **SWB** ME/W 1340/A1/1, 28-5-1985.

74. SAKR, 1982, pp. 159-160

75. MEED, 10-12-1982

76. MEED, 27-3-1981

77. **AT,** 1-1-1983

78. SAKR, 1982, pp. 152-153

79. MEED, 4-6-1982

80. MEED, 2-12-1983

81. MEED, 11-2-1983

82. MEED 15-2-1985

83. MEED, 23-12-1983

84. MEED, 15-4-1983; **MEES,** 19-3-1984

85. MEED, 15-2-1985

86. MEED, 4-1-1986

87. See **MEED,** 30-11-1985

88. **SWB** ME/W 1365/A1/4, 19-11-1985; ME/W 1368/i, 10-12-1985

89. MEED, 30-11-1985; 3-3-1986; 15-3-1986; 7-6-1986

90. SAKR, 1982, pp. 155-158

91. **MEED**, 12-3-1982

92. **MEED**, 14-9-1985

93. **MEED**, 3-5-1986

94. SAKR, 1982, pp. 157-158

95. QNA dispatch 16-3-1983

96. **MEED**, 21-10-1983

97. SPRINGBORG, 1985

98. SAKR, 1982, p. 158

99. QNA dispatch 4-4-1984

100. **Al-Siyasa**, 11-1-1981

101. KUNA dispatch, 22-11-1983; **MEED**, 25-11-1983

102. SAKR, 1982, p. 162; KUNA dispatch 31-7-1982; QNA
dispatch 4-4-1984

103. **Al-Sharq al-Awsat**, 6-10-1980; **MEED**, 25-11-1983;
24-5-1985; **SWB**, ME/W 1340/A1/7, 28-5-1985

104. **Alwaqai Aliraqiya**, 20-3-1985.

105. SAKR, 1982, pp. 156-157

106. **MEED**, 28-11-1980

107. SAKR, 1982, p. 160

108. See **MEED**,   27-3-1981;   15-5-1981;   26-6-1981;
21-8-1981; 13-11-1981; 20-11-1981; 11-12-1981; 3-12-1982;
and the **MEED** contracts lists.

109. **MEED**,   14-1-1983;   29-4-1983;   REUTER dispatch
18-8-1983; the author also draws on his impressions while
working in Iraq in the period under consideration.

110. **MEED**, 16-4-1984

111. **MEED**, 18-1-1986

112. **MEED**, 24-5-1986

113. **MEED**, 29-3-1986

114. **MEED**, 24-7-1981; 2-9-1983

115. **Arab News**, 21-2-1986

116. As for the situation up to 1981, SAKR, 1982, p. 160, reports that many Iraqi engineers were working in the Gulf, particularly in the UAE.

117. **MEED**, 20-1-1984

118. **Al-Siyasa**, 10-8-1981

119. Something must be amiss with the Iraqi figures for export to Bahrain in 1978 and 1979, (table III A.2.a in appendix IV), possibly an inversion: compare with other tables.

120. See for instance **MEED**, 8-1-1982, p. 3; 24-9-1982, p. 10.

121. **MEED**, 15-5-1981

122. **MEED**, 14-8-1981; 18-9-1981

123. **MEED**, 14-8-1981

124. **MEED**, 16-6-1982

125. See **MEED**, 17-12-1982, p. 35; 1-4-1983, p. 16.

126. See **MEED**, 22-4-1983, p. 22.

127. OPECNA dispatch, 13-9-1983

128. **MEED**, 16-12-1983

129. AFESD, 1985

130. SPA dispatch 5-2-1984; **MEED**, 27-4-1984

131. AFESD, 1985

132. See note 67

133. **SWB** ME/W 1339/A1/4, 21-5-1985; ME/W 1358/A1/1, 1-10-1985; **MEED**, 5-10-1985

134. **MEES**, 6-1-1986

135. **MEED**, 2-11-1985; and banking sources

136. **MEES**, 13-1-1986; 20-1-86; 10-3-86; 31-3-86; 14-4-86; 28-4-86; 2-6-86

137. **Al-Siyasa**, 11-1-1981

138. **MEED**, 31-7-1981; 23-6-1982

139. **MEED**, 23-6-1982

140. **The Economist**, 24-7-1982, p. 41

141. **MEED**, 27-7-1982

142. **Al-Watan**, 14-5-1984

143. **MEED**, 4-6-1982

145. **MEED, Iraq Special Report**, October 1982, p. 37

146. **MEED**, 2-12-1983

147. **MEED**, 15-3-1985

148. **MEED**, 15-5-1981; 4-12-1981

149. **MEED**, 18-11-1983; GNA dispatch 20-12-1983; **SWB**, ME/Wi 269/A1/1, 10-1-1984

150. **MEED**, 18-1-1986

151. **BO**, 16-5-1982

152. **MEED**, 22-5-1981

153. **MEJ**, 36, 1982, p. 82

154. **MEED**, 27-5-1983; KUNA dispatch 17-5-1983

155. See also **MEES**, 16-3-1981; **KT**, 4-2-1984; **EN**, 20-3-1983; 31-3-1983; 21-4-1983.

156. See for instance **EN**, 21-4-1983; **BO**, 28-1-1983.

157. QNA dispatch, 9-1-1984; for the 1985 Conference: **SWB**, ME/7844/a/10, 9-1-1985.

158. **Gulf News**, 10-11-1983; KUNA dispatches of 7, 8, and

9-8-1984

159. **MEED**, 4-1-1986

160. SPA dispatches of 13 and 14-6-1984

161. First reported in **MEED**, 2-1-1981. Confirmed to the author by the Iraqi Embassy in London on 3-7-1985.

CONCLUSIONS AND PROSPECTS

Iraqi Foreign Policy and its Determinants since the War

The pre-war evolution towards an internationally 'moderate' position and towards warmer relations with the Arab Gulf states was due to a number of 'pull' factors (or factors making the shift possible), and a number of 'push' factors. The main ones were:

1. 'Pull': (a) financial/economic independence;
           (b) the improved domestic security situation which allowed a more pragmatic policy to be pursued.
2. 'Push': (a) Saddam's domination of policy making;
           (b) a modified ideological stand, stressing the pan-Arabist and non-aligned strands of Baathism, implying an active Iraqi role on the Arab scene;
           (c) the importance attached to the development of economic cooperation and links among Arab countries;
           (d) the concept of using the balance of forces in the world for Iraq's and the non-aligned world's interests.
           (e) the interests of Saddam in building up an alliance with the commercial bourgeoisie and giving more opportunities to private capital: hence the introduction of a measure of **infitah.**

Few significant changes have occurred in these underlying factors since the outbreak of the war. It is clear that some of the financial/economic independence acquired in the 1970s was lost, but this time it was to the Gulf states – which thus reinforced the previous evolution. The concept of the international balance of forces in Iraq's interests was also reinforced due to the war, leading for instance to the re-establishment of diplomatic relations with the US.

The impact of these interlinked factors of indigenous

development and wartime pressures, was particularly
clear in Iraq's stance in the Arab arena. In the pre-War
"National Charter", it had already become evident that
Iraq's pan-Arabism had changed in character: Iraq by
implication accepted the existing state system. In the
course of the war, this shift became even clearer; the
Iraqi Baath has now explicitly rejected the idea of a
single Arab state. In an interview with Kuwaiti
journalists in Morocco, in September 1982, Saddam
declared:

> The Iraqis are now of the opinion that Arab unity
> can only take place after a clear demarcation of
> borders between all countries. We further believe
> that Arab unity must not take place through the
> elimination of the local and national
> characteristics of any Arab country ... The
> question of linking unity to the removal of
> boundaries is no longer acceptable to present Arab
> mentality. It could have been acceptable 10 or 20
> years ago. We have to take into consideration the
> change which the Arab mind and psyche have
> undergone. We must see the world as it is. Any Arab
> would have wished to see the Arab nation as one
> state ... But these are sheer dreams. The Arab
> reality is that the Arabs are now 22 states, and we
> have to behave accordingly. (1)

Determinants of the Iraqi Attitude towards the Arab Gulf States since the War

The continuation of the pre-war trend towards better
relations is to a large extent explained by the above.
Specific determining factors were (a) the fear of
Iran, reinforced during the war; (b) the importance
attached to obtaining Arab Gulf investment in Iraq -
shifting to aid and financing during the war; (c) the
declining importance of ideology in determining Iraqi
policy towards the Six, a decline which accelerated as a
result of the war. Iraq's increasing dependence on the
Gulf states for aid and transshipment diminished its will
and ability to challenge the policies pursued by the Gulf
regimes, e.g. on the formation of the GCC, oil strategy,
or the approach to the peaceful settlement of the
Arab-Israeli conflict (the Fez-plan). This evolution is
clearly observable in the first three years of the war,
and links in with the reformulation of Saddam's view on
pan-Arabism.

The development of the relations with Saudi Arabia was encouraged by the above factors. Ideology as a source of friction all but disappeared. The pre-war state of relations with Kuwait, however, was confirmed. On the one hand, the war dramatically increased Iraq's dependence on the Emirate as an imports-link and aid-donor, and the Iraqis highlighted mutual understanding and cooperation. On the other, the points of friction which existed on the eve of the war, became even more salient. At times, Iraq's realisation of its dependence on Kuwait appeared to make it play the border and islands issues down, but the war situation made Iraqi control over its outlet to the Gulf even more vital, thus causing the matter to remain a serious irritant to relations. As regards the UAE, a distinction must be made between Iraq's attitude to its sympathisers (Abu Dhabi and Ras al-Khaimah), and towards the 'pragmatists' (Dubai and Sharjah). The latter were openly criticized; the former were pressed for support, but when the war became a long-term affair, Iraq appeared to acquiesce in their neutrality, as it did with the other small Gulf states. After all, the main aim of the Iraqis was to end the war.

The Attitudes of the Arab Gulf States towards Iraq

The pre-war change which had occurred in the Six's perception of Iraq, was taken further during the period under consideration, although Kuwait still had reason to be apprehensive over the border question and the islands. Iran was still perceived as a threat, and Iranian declarations had the effect of putting the Gulf states even more firmly in Iraq's camp. But the changing situation on the battlefield strongly influenced their attitudes: whereas the initial Iraqi attack was discreetly welcomed by most in the Six, circumstances after the first blitz dictated a more cautious policy. The direct aim of reducing Khomeini's influence had been achieved, and the war had now turned instead into a military threat, so the states of the Lower Gulf withdrew into a necessity-induced official neutrality. In the wake of Iran's 1986 offensive, they revised their positions only slightly in favour of Iraq, and mainly under the umbrella of the GCC. Kuwait too claimed to be neutral, but in reality kept supporting Iraq; such support was necessary if the turn the war had taken was not to bring Iraq down, and on the whole, Kuwaiti public opinion appears to have been catalysed in favour of Iraq. When Iran crossed the Shatt al-Arab in February 1986, it was Kuwait - most directly threatened - which became Iran's sternest critic, and Iraq's most vocal supporter. Saudi

Arabia stands out by virtue of the firm support it gave
Iraq throughout the nearly six years of the conflict,
recognising the necessity of that support. Though also
preferring a peaceful solution to the conflict (which was
identical to Iraq's desires), and not rejecting Iranian
overtures, the Kingdom never made a secret of its
pro-Iraqi stance, justifying this on grounds of Arabism
and Iraq's wish for peace.

Even though the Six, thus, tilted towards Iraq, they had
no wish to be too closely involved with it. The regime,
after all, was still quite different from the Gulf
monarchies, and its 'conversion' was still fairly recent.
The Gulf war, by tying up both Iraq and Iran, finally
provided the others with an opportunity to form the GCC,
which to some extent formalised the perception of Iraq as
an outsider.

Economic relations between Iraq and the Six developed
further, and extended into the realm of private capital.
This fitted into Saddam's conception of the role economic
links can play in encouraging the evolution towards Arab
Unity. The pre-war trend, thus, was confirmed. The War
had, however, some conflicting effects. It impelled the
regime towards a development and imports boom;
intensified the political will to participate in as many
joint economic schemes as possible; and made the country
even more dependent on Kuwait and Saudi Arabia for
transshipment. Thus, during the first two years of the
war, trade with Kuwait and generally Iraqi activity in
joint schemes increased. But at the same time the war was
creating financial difficulties, which resulted in an
inversion of that trend.

These effects may have cancelled each other out. But the
economic and socio-cultural connection between Iraq and
the Gulf states had now become firmly established,
although temporarily under financial constraints in some
areas.

A general conclusion which emerges from the evidence on
relations between Iraq and the Arab Gulf states, is that
their development was gradual, with perhaps the most
important dividing line falling at the outbreak of the
Iranian Revolution, rather than at the beginning of the
War.

Prospects

At present, with Iraq under serious military and financial pressure, the crucial factor in determining the Gulf states' attitudes towards their northern neighbour is inevitably their perception of the heightened Iranian threat to the region. Under these circumstances, Saudi Arabia and Kuwait will continue to provide political support, as well as material assistance in the form of oil swaps; direct financial transfers (though on a much smaller scale than before 1983); other partial interventions for instance in loan repayments and providing 10 % down-payments to some of Iraq's key suppliers; facilities for transshipment of merchandise imports; and, in the case of Saudi Arabia, an outlet for Iraqi oil exports through IPSA-1 and 2, in effect the most eloquent expression of political support. Moreover, it seems clear that Saudi Arabia has been won round to supporting Iraq's strategy of putting pressure on Iran's oil-export channels. Short of dropping the Iraqi regime altogether, such pressure would indeed seem the only means whereby Iran might be brought to the negotiating table. At the same time Syria would have to be persuaded to resume relations with Iraq. This latter aim has been and is being pursued.

The other four states are likely to remain basically neutral, after their initial statements criticising Iran for its 1986 offensives. Minor variations among them in public stances notwithstanding, they hope forlornly that Iran can be persuaded to accept peace - but are not in a position to do much else. Expressions of their tilt towards Iraq, in the face of the Iranian military threat, will be reserved for the GCC forum, which provides at least some kind of umbrella.

The development of economic relations between Iraq and the GCC in general, and with Kuwait and Saudi Arabia in particular, is likely to continue, to the benefit of all parties.

As for the longer-term prospects, if or when the war will have come to an end, the change in Iraqi foreign policy orientation and behaviour appears real, and thus has implications beyond the period of war. The economic and socio-cultural links, too, not only fit into a foreign policy concept that looks at them on a long-term basis, but have developed to an extent wich appears almost structural. Iraq's choice of a degree of **infitah** (regardless of the relative importance of the reasons listed earlier) also implies a long-term commitment. This

is not compatible with a renewed 'radical' attitude
towards the Six. Moreover, it would be unlikely that
Iraq would feel confident enough to attempt any new
adventures in the near future. Alienating the Gulf states
would mean writing off valuable potential supporters in
case of renewed tension with Iran.

Iran remains a potential threat to the Gulf states. The
evolution of Iranian foreign policy will set the context
for future relations between the Six and Iran. Most
likely a modus vivendi will be reached. As Sultan Qabus
has said: there is no alternative to peaceful
co-existence between Persians and Arabs. The Gulf states,
then, intent on preserving their domestic security, will
try to maintain friendly relations with both Iraq and
Iran, while at the same time remaining aloof from too
strong an involvement with either. The 'Arab connection'
will not be denied, and although Iraq will not be
accepted into the GCC (probably the main lasting memorial
of the war), structural links should continue to develop.

NOTE TO CONCLUSION

1. Repeated on Baghdad's **Sawt   al-Jamahir,**   on 10-9-1982;
quoted in HELMS, 1984, p. 115.

———————

A P P E N D I C E S

1.
The presence in the Arab homeland of any foreign troops or military forces shall be rejected and no facilities for the use of Arab territory shall be extended to them in any form or under any pretext or cover. Any Arab regime that fails to comply with this principle shall be proscribed and boycotted both economically and politically, as well as politically opposed by all available means.

2.
The recourse to armed force by one Arab state against another Arab state shall be prohibited, and any dispute arising between Arab states shall be resolved by peaceful means in accordance with the principles of joint Arab action and the higher Arab interest.

3.
The principle embodied in Article 2 shall apply to the relations of the Arab nation and its constituent states with neighbouring countries, with recourse to armed force in any disputes prohibited except in case of self-defense or the defense of sovereignty against threats that affect the security and vital interests of the Arab states.

4.
All the Arab states shall collaborate in opposing any aggression or violation by any foreign power directed against the territorial sovereignty of any Arab state or the waging of war against any Arab state. All the Arab states shall act together in facing up to and repelling such aggression or violation by every available means including military action, collective political and economic boycotts, or action in other fields as the need arises and in accordance with the dictates of the national interest.

5.
The Arab states reaffirm their adherence to international law and practice in so far as concerns the use of air space, waterways and land routes by any states not in a state of war with any Arab state.

6.
The Arab states shall steer clear of the arena of international conflicts and wars, and shall maintain strict neutrality and non-alignment vis-a-vis any party to a conflict or war, provided that none of the parties to such conflicts and wars shall violate Arab territorial sovereignty or the established rights of the Arab states as guaranteed by international law and practice. The Arab states shall prohibit any involvement by their armed forces, partially or totally, in wars or armed disputes in the area or outside it on

behalf of any state or foreign party.

7.

The Arab states undertake to establish close economic ties between each other in such a manner as to make possible the creation of a common foundation for an advanced and unified Arab economic structure.

8.

In putting forward the principles of this charter, Iraq reaffirms its readiness to assume the commitments implicit in it towards all Arab states or any party that adheres to it, and is prepared to discuss it with the other Arab states and would welcome any suggestions that would reinforce its effectiveness.

APPENDIX II
SUMMARY OF PHASES IN THE WAR

I. **IRAQI OFFENSIVE :   22-9-1980   TO OCTOBER 1980**

(a) The Iraqi blitz :   22-9-1980 to   early October (1).
(b) Slow advance :   October 1980.
           culminating in the capture of Khorramshahr on 24-10   (2).

II. **STALEMATE :   NOVEMBER 1980   TO   LATE SEPTEMBER   1981**

(a) Stalemate, still with Iraqi initiative :
                         November 1980 to   late March 1981.
    The end of this phase came when, after the Iranians
    rejected the UN cease fire and withdrawal appeal which
    was accepted by Iraq, Saddam decided to try and take
    Susangerd but failed (19/20-3-1981) (3).
(b) Stalemate :   April 1981 to   late September 1981.
    the beginning of which phase was indicated by the Iranian
    raid destroying 46 warplanes at Iraq's al-Walid base, on
    4-4-1981 (4).

III. **THE IRANIAN COUNTEROFFENSIVE :   28-9-1981   TO   JUNE 1982**

(a) Iranians recover ground :
                         28-9-1981 to   March 1982.
    On 28-9-1981 The Iranians broke the siege of Abadan (5).
    In a campaign from late November to December, 7, Bustan
    was recaptured (6).
(b) Iranian offensive : 22-3-1982 to   June 1982.
    On 22-3-982, Iran launched its attack in the Dezful-
      Shush region, a disaster for Iraq (7).
    8-4-1982 : Syria closes the border with Iraq.
    10-4-1982 : Syrian pipeline closed (8).
    11-4-1982 : start of economic austerity announced (9).
    30-4-1982 : new Iranian offensive, driving the Iraqis
      back to the border, between Husseiniya and Khorram-
      shahr (10).
    24-5-1982 : Khorramshahr recaptured (11).
    20-6-1982 : Saddam announces the Iraqi withdrawal to
      the international borders "within ten days" (12).

IV. **STALEMATE, IRAN HAS THE INITIATIVE :   12-7-1982 TO FEBRUARY
     1984**

- The war is carried into Iraq, from the 12-6-1982 "Ramadhan"
  Offensive against Basra (13), to the 22-2-1984 invasion of the
  Huwaiza marshes, when Majnoon was captured (14).
- But at the same time, Iraqi morale and organisation appear to
  improve, leading to a renewed stalemate.

- This is brought about also by the resumption of Soviet arms deliveries (15).
- 12-8-1982 : Iraq declares an exclusion zone in the northern Gulf, including Kharg (16).
- From mid-1983 Iraq begins to prepare for the internationalised phase of the war. In May Tariq Aziz visits Paris where he also meets with US Secretary of State Schultz. From fall 1983, lays the groundwork for the actual internationalisation of the conflict. The **Super Etendards** are delivered in October and the threats of July- August 1982 are followed up by some attacks on Kharg. International concern is further raised by the missile attacks on civilian tar- gets and the use of gas in trying to turn the tide of the Huweiza offensive (17).

V.   INTERNATIONALISED CONFLICT AND STALEMATE :   SPRING   1984 TO JANUARY 1986

(a)
- 27-2-1984 : Iraq declares the start of the siege of Kharg (18).
- From late March the attacks on tankers begin; in earnest from April, 18 and 25, when resp. a Panamian tanker and the **Safina al-Arab** are attacked (19).
- Iraqi attacks bring Iranian retaliation on tankers with Arab oil.
- This in turn leads to a hardening in the position of the GCC and a GCC-sponsored UN condemnation of Iran for those attacks. On June, 5, 1984, Saudi fighters shoot down an Iranian plane (20).
- The situation on the front, and in the international context (aid, supplies) favours the Iraqis in a no-end stalemate.

(b)
- Spring 1985: a War of the Cities breaks out, for some three months.
- from 15-8-1985, attacks on Kharg become more damaging, bringing Iranian oil exports down and continuously hampering them (21).
- Simultaneously, Iran starts a campaign of seizing Iraq-bound vessels in or just outside the Gulf.
- Oil prices begin sliding to c. $ 26 /barrel by end 1985, and below $ 20 /barrel by February 1986.

VI. IRAQ UNDER PRESSURE

- 9-2-1986: Iran advances into Iraq and captures Fao (22).
- 25-2-1986: Iran attacks in the north (23).
- Iraq manages to stop the advance and to regain some positions, but remains under pressure (24).
- Early June 1986: Khomeini calls for total mobilisation (25).
- Iran keeps stopping ships suspected of carrying goods for

Iraq.
- The tanker war escalates further, with a first quarter figure
  for 1986 of 28 confirmed hits, as against 40 for all 1985
  (26).
- Oil prices plummet to $ 15 / barrel and below. Iraq as a
  result experiences severe financial difficulties.

———————

NOTES

1. **Time**, 13-10-1980, p. 12.
2. NONNEMAN, 1984a, p. 36.
3. HIRO, 1984, p. 6.
4. Ibid., p. 7.
5. **The Times**, 23-9-1983, p. 10.
6. Ibid.
7. HIRO, 1984, p. 8.
8. Ibid.
9. Ibid.
10. Ibid.
11. IBID.
12. **The Times**, 23-9-1983, p. 10.
13. Ibid.
14. NONNEMAN, 1984a, pp. 37-38; 1984b, p. 557.
15. HIRO, 1984, p. 10.
16. **The Times**, 23-9-1983, p. 10.
17. NONNEMAN, 1984a, pp. 38-40; and HIRO, 1984, p. 11.
18. **Gulf Daily News**, 28-2-1984.
19. HIRO, 1984, p. 13.
20. NONNEMAN, 1984b, pp. 558, 561.
21. **MEED**, 7-9-1985; 14-9-1985; **Gulf Daily News**, 29-9-1985.
22. **MEED**, 15-2-1986.
23. **MEED**, 8-3-1986.
24. Several issues of **MEED**, **FT**, fron February to June 1986.
25. **MEED**, 7-6-1986.
26. **MEES**, 7-4-1986.

APPENDIX III

LIST OF RECORDED HIGH-LEVEL VISITS BETWEEN IRAQ AND THE GCC STATES, 1980 - FEBRUARY 1986

NOTE:

- Under high-level visits we understand Minister-level or higher. Visits of lower-ranked officials are also included if they carry messages from that higher level and are received as such. An exception can be made when it is felt that a particular visit/message may have had special importance.

- The series starts before the war, in order to make comparison possible.

- Roman numbers on the left indicate each of the 6 periods of the war (See App. II).

- **symbols:**　　 > : going to/ addressed at
　　　　　　　　 < : from
　　　　　　　　 + : together with
　　　　　　　　 M : Minister
　　　　　　　 FM : Foreign Minister
　　　　　　 MCA : Minister of State for Cabinet Affairs
　　　　　　 Sh. : Shaikh
　　　　　 mess. : message
　　　　　　 del. : delivered by
　　　　　　　 w. : with
　　　　　　　 SH : Saddam Hussein
　　　　 S al-F : Prince Saud al-Faysal
　　　　　　 TYR : Taha Yassin Ramadhan
　　　　　 rcvd : received
　　　　　　　 VP : Vice President

- NORMAL PRINT indicates visits from Iraq;
  BOLD PRINT indicates visits **to** Iraq.

SAUDI ARABIA	KUWAIT	BAHRAIN	QATAR	U A E	OMAN
25-2-1980 Izzat + delegation rcvd by Prince Fahd+ Abdullah + Sultan (1)	25-2-1980 PM > Baghdad for border question (2)	29-2-1980 2-day visit of Sh. Hamad b. Isa (3)			
	early May Sh. Saad > SH + Izzat (5 days) (4)				
					26-5-1980 Q. Zawawi brings mess. of Qabus > SH (5)
				2-6-1980 Sh. Saqr (RAK) > SH, Izzat (6)	
				29-7-1980 Sh. Suroor as envoy of Zayid (7)	
5-8-1980 SH + Tariq Aziz > Khalid + Fahd + Saud al-Faysal (2 days) (8)	10-8-1980 mess. < Amir (9)			23-8-1980 Zayid mess. > SH, del. Sh. Suroor (10)	
mid-September Iraqi envoy > Riyad (12)		2-9-1980 PM Sh. Khalifa (11)			
I					1st week of the war: Iraqi envoy (12 b)
				27-10-1980 SH mess. > Zayid, del. H. Alwan (13)	
II				13-11-1980 SH mess. > Zayid, del. S. Shakir (14) Saddam	(14 b for Qabus)
Amman Summit :	all Six	heads of State	meet with		
30-12-1980 S al-F + Algerian PM + Klibi (16)	28-12-1980 PM > SH (15)				
	January 1981 TYR mess.> Sh. Sabah del. Dep. Trade M (16b)				
	10-2-1981 S. Shakir: border talks on Iraqi request (17)				

SAUDI ARABIA	KUWAIT				
6-4-1981 S. Hammadi: SH mess. > King Khalid (19)	5-4-1981 S. Hammadi: SH mess. > Amir (18)				
5-8-1981 mess. < Khalid + Fahd > SH, del. Educ. M (21)	23-7-1981 Dep. Int. M. letter > Kuwaiti counterp.(20)				
11-8-1981 Khalid mess. > SH del.Plann. M (22)					
25-9-1981 Abdullah in Baghdad meets SH (23)					
III					
2-11-1981 Abduh Yamani > SH (24)	9-12-1981 Amir mess. > SH del.MCA (verbal) (25)				
26-12-1981 Nayif > Baghdad for border agreement (26)	16-1-1982 Amir mess. > SH del. MCA (27)				
18-1-1982 Abdullah > SH (28)					
9-2-1982 TYR w. SH mess. > Khalid. Talks w. Fahd + S al-F. (29)					7-4-1982 Zayid mess. > SH, del. M of St. FA (31)
3-4-1982 Sultan > SH, w. mess. < Fahd (32)					
25-4-1982					

SAUDI ARABIA	KUWAIT	BAHRAIN	QATAR	U A E	OMAN
Izzat: SH mess. > top 4 + S. al-F. (33)					
IV 18-7-1982 TYR > Fahd (34)	TYR > Amir (35)				
9-10-1982 S. Shakir: SH mess. > Fahd. Talks w. Fahd + Abdullah + S al-F. (36)	20-10-1982 S. Shakir: SH mess. > Amir (37)				
5/6-12-1982 VP T.M.Maaruf: talks w. Abdullah + Sultan (38)					
15-1-1983 **Abdullah > Baghdad** (39)					
17-1-1983 **Abdullah > Baghdad** (40)					
18-1-1983 SH > Fahd (41)					
19-1-1983 **Abdullah w. SH >** **Baghdad** (42)			26-2-1983 Oil M Taqi (43)		
27-2-1983 FM Undersec. > S al-F. (44)					

SAUDI ARABIA	KUWAIT	BAHRAIN			
1-8-1983 TYR: SH mess. > Fahd (45)	2-8-1983 TYR : SH mess. > Amir (46)			3-8-1983 SH mess. > Zayid, del. special advisor for military aff. (47)	
	3-9-1983 Sh. Sabah (MF) (48)		10-9-1983 FM > T. Aziz (49)		
			See UAE	8-10-1983 Zayid stopover to att. meeting w. SH + Qatari FM (> Damascus) (50)	
20-10-1983 Fahd mess. > SH del. Al-Qusaibi (51)		22-10-1983 TYR: SH mess. > Amir (52)	22-10-1983 TYR: SH mess. >Amir (53)		22-10-1983 TYR: SH mess. > Sultan (54)
1-11-1983 SH mess. > Fahd, del. Oil M Taqi (55)					
22-11-1983 Abdullah 1 day visit (56)					
25-12-1983 Abdullah (unannounced) (57)					
	28-1-1984 Oil M. Taqi > Kuwaiti Oil M. (58)				
				22-2-1984 SH mess. > Zayid, del. Oil M Taqi (59)	
V 14-3-1984: all Foreign Ministers in Baghdad for Arab League emergency meeting.					
29-4-1984 Tariq Aziz > Riyadh (60)					

SAUDI ARABIA	KUWAIT	BAHRAIN	QATAR	U A E	OMAN
30-5-1984 SH mess. > Fahd, del. T. Aziz (61)	2-6-1984 SH mess. > Amir, del. T. Aziz (62)				
	4-7-1984 T. Aziz talks w. FM (63)				
	7-7-1984 T. Aziz talks w. FM (64)				
8-8-1984 Izzat + delegation (see Kuwait) (66)	4-8-1984 Izzat + high delegation SH mess. > Amir, and high level talks (65)	5-8-1984 Izzat + delegation (see Kuwait) (66)	6-8-1984 Izzat + delegation (see Kuwait)(67)	6-8-1984 Izzat + delegation (see Kuwait) (68)	7-8-1984 Izzat + delegation (see Kuwait) (69)
20-9-1984 S. Shakir > Fahd (71)					
7-11-1984 SH mess. > Fahd, del. Oil M Taqi (72)	12-11-1984 Sh. Saad (2-day visit) (73)				
	20-11-1984 S. Shakir: talks w. FM (74)				
29-12-1984 Dep. Def. & Aviat.M rcvd by SH (75)	19-1-1985 Q.A.Taqi > Amir, w. SH mess. (76)				
25-1-1985 S al-F. meets SH (part of AL comm) (77)					
19-2-1985 Pr. Bandar w. mess. < Fahd > SH (ex USA) (78)					

SAUDI ARABIA	KUWAIT	BAHRAIN	QATAR	U A E	OMAN
	19-3-1985 FM Sh. Sabah al-Ahmad (79)				
20-7-1985 T. Aziz > Riyadh to discuss call for Rabat Summit (80)	22-7-1985 to 24-7-1985 : T.Y. al-Ali (FM Undersec.) on Gulf tour to discuss the same issue (81)				
	17-8-1985 RCC member Hashim Aqrawi + del. (82)				
8-9-1985 Izzat > Fahd (83) 12-9-1985 Abdullah (in "Comm. for clearing Arab atmosphere"). (84)					
30-10-1985 T. Aziz w. mess. < SH (86) 2-11-1985 T. Aziz (87)	30-10-1985 see Saudi Arabia				28/29-10-1985 Hamid Alwan (Presid. Adviser For. Aff.) (81) 11-11-1985 M. of St. For. Aff. Yusuf Alawi > SH w. mess. > Qabus (88)
30-12-1985 T.Aziz > Fahd (89) 13-1-1986 S. Shakir > 2 Dep. Interior Ministers (90)					

SAUDI ARABIA	KUWAIT	BAHRAIN	QATAR	U A E	OMAN
VI 9/10-2-1986 Izzat + A.Q. Taqi > Abdullah, Sultan, Yamani, (Fahd?) (91) 12-2-1986 A.L. 7-man committee in Baghdad, incl. S. al-F. and Sh. Sabah al-Ahmad (92) 17-2-1986 S. al-F. and Sh . Sabah return to Baghdad from Damascus (93) 22-2-1986 S. al-F. > SH Asad (94)	23-2-1986 A.Q. Taqi > Amir, Sh. Ali Khalifa w. mess. < SH (95)				

NOTES TO CHRONOLOGY OF VISITS

1. **Saudi Gazette**, 26-2-1980
2. HEARD-BEY, 1983, p. 69
3. **MEED**, 29-2-1980, p. 28
4. **AT**, 8-5-1980, and the **Sawt al-Jamahir** at 10-5-1980, quoted in **SWB**, ME/6471/A/6-8, 12-5-1980.
5. **Al-Siyasa**, 27-5-1980
6. **EN**, 3-6-1980; **BO**, 4-6-1980
7. MOSS-HELMS, 1983, p. 81
8. **MEES**, 11-8-1980; XINHUA dispatch 6-8-1980
9. MOSS-HELMS, 1983, p. 81
10. ibid.
11. ibid.; **SWB**, ME/6515/A/2, 5-9-1980
12. HELLER, 1983, p. 4
12b.According to the Omani Undersecretary for Foreign Affairs, quoted in **MEED**, 21-11-1980, p. 3.
13. WAM dispatch 27-10-1980
14. **SWB**, 13-11-1980
14b. **Al-Siyasa**, 3-12-1980
15. See **MEJ**, 35 (1981), p. 221
16. ibid.
17. **AT**, 12-2-1981
18. XINHUA dispatch 5-4-1981
19. ibid.
20. **Al-Siyasa**, 23-7-1981
21. REUTER dispatch 5-8-1981
22. REUTER dispatch, 11-8-1981
23. **Arab News**, 26-9-1981
24. See **MEJ**, 36 (1982), p. 227
25. REUTER dispatch 9-12-1981
26. AFP dispatch 26-12-1981; **KEESING'S**, 1982, p. 31523
27. REUTER dispatch 16-1-1982
28. See **MEJ**, 36 (1982), p. 402
29. KUNA dispatch 9-2-1982
30. See **MEJ**, 36 (1982), p. 402
31. REUTER dispatch 7-4-1982
32. **MEED**, 9-4-1982, p. 3
33. SPA dispatch 25-4-1982
34. SPA dispatch 18-7-1982
35. id.
36. KUNA dispatch 9-10-1982
37. KUNA dispatch 20-10-1982
38. SPA dispatches of 5,6-12-1982
39. **MEED**, 21-1-1983; AFP dispatch 15-1-1983
40. QNA dispatch 18-1-1983
41. SPA dispatch 18-1-1983
42. KUNA dispatch 19-1-1983
43. SPA dispatch 26-2-1983
44. SPA dispatch 27-2-1983

45. QNA dispatch 2-8-1983
46. id.
47. REUTER dispatch 3-8-1983
48. QNA dispatch 3-9-1983
49. KUNA dispatch 10-9-1983
50. QNA dispatch 8-10-1983; **SWB**, ME/7461/A/6, 11-10-1983
51. REUTER dispatch 20-10-1983
52. KUNA dispatch 22-10-1983; REUTER dispatch 23-10-1983
53. id.
54. id.
55. REUTER dispatch 1-11-1983
56. SPA dispatch 22-11-1983
57. INA dispatch, 25-12-1983
58. **SWB**, ME/7630/A/10, 30-4-1984
59. KUNA dispatch 22-2-1984
60. **SWB**, ME/7630/A/10, 30-4-1984
61. KUNA dispatch 31-5-1984
62. KUNA dispatch 2-6-1984
63. KUNA dispatch 4-7-1984
64. QNA dispatch 9-7-1984
65. KUNA dispatch 4-8-1984; SPA dispatch 4-8-1984; **BO**, 6-8-1984
66. SPA dispatches of 5-8-1984; REUTER dispatch 5-8-1984
67. SPA dispatch 6-8-1984; REUTER dispatch 6-8-1984
68. SPA dispatch 6-8-1984
69. KUNA dispatch 7-8-1984
70. SPA dispatches of 8-8-1984; **BO**, 9-8-1984
71. **SWB**, ME/7756/A/18, 24-9-1984
72. **SWB**, ME/7796/A/10, 9-11-1984
73. **SWB**, ME/7806/A/7, 21-11-1984
74. **SWB**, ME/7806/i, 21-11-1984
75. **SWB**, ME/7838/A/9, 2-1-1985
76. **SWB**, ME/7855/A/6, 22-1-1985
77. **MEED**, 25-1-1985
78. **SWB**, ME/7884/A/8, 25-2-1985
79. **MEJ**, Summer 1985, p. 372
80. **MEED**, 27-7-1985, p. 16
81. ibid.
82. **SWB**, ME/8035/A/9, 21-8-1985
83. **SWB**, ME/8055/A/7, 13-9-1985
84. **SWB**, ME/8056/i, 14-9-1985
85. **SWB**, ME/8099/A/6, 4-11-1985
86. ibid.
87. **SWB**, ME/8104/A/9, 9-11-1985
88. **SWB**, ME/8106/i, 12-11-1985
89. **SWB**, ME/8145/i, 1-1-1986
90. **Arab News**, 13-1-1986
91. **Arab News**, 10-2-1986; **EN**, 10-2-1986; **Gulf News**, 10-2-1986;
92. **SWB**, ME/8184/A/7, 15-2-1986
93. **Arab News**, 18-2-1986
94. **Jordan Times**, 24-2-1986
95. **Jordan Times**, 24-2-1986; **Saudi Gazette**, 23-2-1986

APPENDIX IV

TRADE-FLOWS BETWEEN IRAQ AND THE ARAB GULF STATES

NOTE:

For each trade-relationship 8 tables are presented, 4 for each way. Of those 4, 2 consist of figures for the exports of country A to country B (once in US $ data, once in local currency), and the other 2 consist of figures for country B's imports from country A. Thus for each 'flow' quadruple evidence is given. This seemed necessary given the incompleteness, unreliability and, often, the mutual incompatibility of existing data. Rather than forcing all those diverse data into one estimate, and making errors and false assumptions, it was preferred to make each of the four types of data as complete as possible in their own right, and allow the reader to contrast them. Conclusions that can be drawn, are drawn in Chapter VIII, section E.3.

An example: The Iraqi-Saudi trade relationship is treated in the following 8 tables:
A. IRAQ TO SAUDI ARABIA
   1. IN US $
      a. Iraqi Exports to Saudi Arabia.
      b. Saudi Imports from Iraq.
   2. IN LOCAL CURRENCY
      a. Iraqi Exports to Saudi Arabia, in ID.
      b. Saudi Imports from Iraq, in SR.
B. SAUDI ARABIA TO IRAQ
   1. IN US $
      a. Iraqi Imports from Saudi Arabia.
      b. Saudi Exports to Iraq.
   2. IN LOCAL CURRENCY
      a. Iraqi Imports from Saudi Arabia, in ID.
      b. Saudi Exports to Iraq, in SR.

In each case the share of trade with the partner country in total trade is given, and where possible (in the local currency tables) also the share in trade with the Arab world, since that may be a fairer comparison.

NOTE: "SESTRCIC, Summary Statistics" stands for:
      Statistical, Economic and Social Training and Research Centre for the Islamic Countries (ICO)(Ankara): **Summary Statistics. Basic Socio-economic indicators for Islamic Countries, 1980.**

NOTE: - stands for: "negligible"
       ... stands for: "not available".
NOTE: Export figures are fob, Import figures are c+f or cif

I.   IRAQ - SAUDI ARABIA

A. IRAQ TO SAUDI ARABIA

1. IN US $ MILLIONS

a. Iraqi Exports to Saudi Arabia, 1976 - 1984

	Exp. to Saudi Arabia	Total Exports	%
1976	1.7 (d) (3.1 e; 8 b)	8,518 (b) (8,296 e)	0.02 (0.04)
1977	2.2 (d) (3 a)10	10,372 (a)	0.02
1978	1.8 (d) (1.4 c)	11,979 (a)	0.02
1979	6 (a)	20,320 (a)	0.03
1980	3 (a)	28,484 (a)	0.01
1981	2 (a)	11,631 (a)	0.02
1982	2 (a)	10,649 (a)	0.02
1983	5 (f)	8,881 (a)	0.06
1984	25 (g)	...	

b. Saudi Imports from Iraq, 1976 - 1984

	Imports from Iraq	Total Imports (*)	%
1976	3 (e) (9 b)	11,812 (e) (8,694 b)	0.03 (0.1)
1977	3 (b)	14,654 (b)	0.02
1978	2 (b)	20,349 (b)	0.01
1979	7 (b)	24,257 (b)	0.03
1980	3 (b)	30,166 (b)	0.01
1981	2 (b)	35,268 (b)	0.01
1982	2 (a)	40,653 (a)	0.00
1983	5 (f)	39,181 (f)	0.01
1984	...	33,368 (f)	...

a- IMF **DTS Yb** 1984   d- UN **Yb ITS 1982**
b- id.   1983   e- SESTRCIC, **Summary Statistics**
c- SAKR, 1982, p. 162   f- IMF **DTS Yb** 1985
                               g- **MEED,** 7-12-1985
*- Striking difference with (Saudi   ?) figures   quoted   in UN **MBS,** Vol.
39,5: May 1985; for instance 1978: 20,424; 1979: 24,462; 1980: 30,211;
1981: 35,244; 1982: 40,654.

2. IRAQ TO SAUDI ARABIA, IN LOCAL CURRENCY
a. **Iraqi Exports to Saudi Arabia, in ID 1000, 1976 - 1984**

	Exp. to SA	Tot. Exp.	%	Exp. to Arab W.	%
1976	503 (a)	2,738,100 (c)	0.02	8,749 (a)	5.57
1977	663 (a)	2,849,600 (c)	0.02	10,734 (a)	6.18
1978	573 (b)	3,266,400 (c)	0.02	15,809 (b)	3.62
1979	442 (b)	6,329,000 (c)	0.01	17,267 (b)	2.56
1980	739 (b)	7,760,300 (c)	0.01	10,475 (b)	7.05
1981	...	3,109,700 (c)		...	
1982	...	3,055,700 (c)		...	
1983	...	...		...	
1984	...	...		...	

b. **Saudi Imports from Iraq, in SR 1000, 1976 - 1984**

	Imp. fr. Iraq	Tot. Imports	%	Imp. fr. Arab W.	%
1976	29,993 (d)	30,690,693 (d)	0.01	7,486,660 (d)	0.40
1977	11,687 (d)	51,661,994 (d)	0.02	7,411,785 (d)	0.16
1978	5,074 (d)	69,179,707 (d)	0.01	3,081,189 (d)	0.16
1979	23,383 (d)	82,223,289 (d)	0.03	3,874,866 (d)	0.60
1980	9,644 (d)	100,349,633 (d)	0.01	4,338,735 (d)	0.22
1981	7,143 (d)	119,297,671 (d)	0.01	5,373,226 (d)	0.13
1982	5,572 (e)	139,335,073 (e)	0.00	5,223,453 (e)	0.11
1983	17,106 (e)	135,417,174 (e)	0.01	4,597,663 (e)	0.37
1984	91,600 (f)	...		...	

a- Rep. of Iraq, Ministry of Planning, CSO, **Annual Abstract of Statistics, 1978**
b- id., **1981**
c- UN **Yb ITS 1982**
d- Saudi Arabia, **Foreign Trade Statistics 1978 AD**, Vol. 1; and **1981 AD**
e- Kingdom of Saudi Arabia, Ministry of Nat. Econ., C.D.S., **Foreign Trade. Kingdom's import Statistics 1983 AD**
f- **MEED**, 7-12-1985

B. SAUDI ARABIA TO IRAQ

1. IN US $ MILLIONS

a. **Iraqi imports from Saudi Arabia, 1976 – 1984**

	Imports from SA	Total Imports	%
1976	...	3,900 (b)	...
1977	...	4,481 (a)	...
1978	...	4,212 (a)	...
1979	7 (a)	9,868 (a)	0.07
1980	22 (a)	13,759 (a)	0.16
1981	54 (a)	20,518 (a)	0.26
1982	59 (a)	21,577 (a)	0.27
1983	47 (f)	12,500 (g)-15,500 (h)	0.38 - 0.31
1984	...	11,000 (g)-12,492 (i)	...

b. **Saudi exports to Iraq, 1976 – 1984**

	Exports to Iraq	Total Exports	%
1976	–	...	
1977	–	...	
1978	2 (b)	37,186 (b)	0.01
1979	6 (b)	58,652 (b)	0.01
1980	20 (b)	102,012 (b)	0.02
1981	49 (b)	113,230 (b)	0.04
1982	53 (a)	75,839 (a)	0.07
1983	43 (f)	49,989 (f)	0.09
1984	...	...	...

a- IMF **DTS Yb,** 1984
b- id. 1983
d- UN **Yb ITS 1982.**
f- **IMF** DTS Yb, **1985**
g- MEED **estimate (10-8-1985, p. 23)**
h- **EIU estimate:** EIU QER Iraq Annual Supplement **1985, p. 18**
i- ibid., **p. 17**

2. SAUDI ARABIA TO IRAQ, IN LOCAL CURRENCY

a. Iraqi Imports from Saudi Arabia, in ID 1000, 1976 - 1984

	Imp. from SA	Total Imports	%	Imports fr. Arab W.	%
1976	23 (a)	1,150,898 (a)	0.00	20,605 (a)	0.11
1977	48 (a)	1,323,153 (a)	0.00	22,479 (a)	0.21
1978	97 (b)	1,473,575 (b)	0.01	25,005 (b)	0.39
1979	355 (b)	1,738,906 (b)	0.02	52,213 (b)	0.68
1980	143 (b)	4,208,079 (b)	0.00	69,560 (b)	0.21
1981	...	...		...	...
1982	...	...		...	...
1983	...	...		...	...
1984	...	...		...	...

b. Saudi Exports to Iraq, in SR 1000, 1976 - 1984

	Exports to Iraq	Total Exports	%	Exports to Arab W.	%
1976	1,204	135,153,518	0.00	4,443,118	0.03
1977	630	153,208,570	0.00	5,947,191	0.01
1978	6,048	138,242,009	0.00	5,274,718	0.11
1979	22,090	213,183,387	0.01	8,697,077	0.25
1980	72,236	362,885,751	0.02	14,264,420	0.51
1981	147,834	405,480,997	0.04	20,531,314	0.72
1982	...	271.090,000 (f)		...	...
1983	...	162,290,000 (f)		...	...
1984	...	...		...	...

All figures in table b, except (f), from : Saudi Arabia, **Foreign Trade Statistics 1978 AD;** and **1981 AD.**

a- Rep. of Iraq, Ministry of Planning, CSO, **Annual Abstract of Statistics, 1978**
b- id., 1981
f- UN **MBS**, Vol. 39,5: May 1985

II.   IRAQ - KUWAIT

A.   IRAQ TO KUWAIT

1. IN US $ MILIONS

a. Iraqi exports to Kuwait, 1976 - 1984

	Exports to Kuwait	Total Exports	%
1976	9 (a)	8,518 (a)	0.11
1977	9 (b)	10,372 (b)	0.09
1978	10 (b)	11,979 (b)	0.08
1979	6 (b)	20,320 (b)	0.03
1980	6 (b)	28,484 (b)	0.02
1981	6 (b)	11,631 (b)	0.05
1982	11 (b)	10,649 (b)	0.10
1983	8 (c)	8,881 (c)	0.09
1984	...	9,681 (c)	...

b. Kuwaiti Imports from Iraq, 1976 - 1984

	Imports from Iraq	Total Imports	%
1976	10 (a)	3,324 (a)	0.30
1977	10 (a)	4,843 (a)	0.21
1978	11 (a)	4,604 (a)	0.24
1979	7 (a)	5,198 (a)	0.13
1980	7 (a)	6,533 (a)	0.11
1981	6 (b)	7,038 (b)	0.09
1982	12 (b)	8,285 (c)	0.14
1983	9 (c)	8,126 (c)	0.11
1984	...	7,641 (c)	...

a. IMF **DTS Yb** 1983
b. id., 1984
c. id., 1985

2. IRAQ TO KUWAIT, IN LOCAL CURRENCY

a. Iraqi exports to Kuwait, in ID 1000,   1976 - 1984

	Exp. to Kuwait	Total Exports	%	Exp. to Arab W.	%
1976	2490 (a)	2,738,100 (c)	0.09	8,749 (a)	28.46
1977	3359 (a)	2,849,600 (c)	0.12	10,734 (a)	31.29
1978	4364 (b)	3,266,400 (c)	0.13	15,809 (b)	27.60
1979	1952 (b)	6,329,000 (c)	0.03	17,067 (b)	11.30
1980	1629 (b)	7,760,300 (c)	0.02	10,475 (b)	15.55
1981	...	3,109,700 (c)		...	
1982	...	3,055,700 (c)		...	
1983	...	...		...	
1984	...	...		...	

b. Kuwaiti Imports from Iraq, in KD 1000,   1976 - 1984

	Imp. fr. Iraq	Total Imports	%	Imp. fr. Arab W.	%
1976	2,963 (e)	971,933 (e)	0.30	24,298 (e)	12.19
1977	2,810 (d)	1,387,035 (d)	0.20	33,065 (d)	8.50
1978	2,979 (d)	1,265,182 (d)	0.24	45,155 (d)	6.60
1979	1,799 (d)	1,437,023 (d)	0.13	55,561 (d)	3.24
1980	1,827 (d)	1,764,902 (d)	0.10	65,176 (d)	2.80
1981	1,689 (d)	1,945,386 (d)	0.09	65,608 (d)	2.57
1982	...	2,385,000 (f)		...	
1983	...	...		...	
1984	...	...		...	

a. Rep. of Iraq, Ministry of Planning, CSO, **Annual Abstract of Statistics 1978**
b. id., **1981**
c. UN **Yb ITS 1982**
d. Kuwait, Ministry of Planning, CSO, **Annual Stat. Abstract 1984.**
e. id., **1982**
f. UN **MBS**, Vol. 39,5, May 1985

B.   KUWAIT TO IRAQ

1. IN US $ MILLIONS

a. **Iraqi Imports from Kuwait,   1976 – 1984**

	Imports fr. Kuwait	Total Imports (*)	%
1976	13 (b)	3,900 (b)	0.33
1977	6 (a)	4,481 (a)	0.13
1978	6 (a) (87.6c)	4,212 (a)	0.14 (2.08)
1979	250 (a)	9.868 (a)	2.53
1980	462 (a)	13,759 (a)	3.36
1981	1,115 (a)	20,518 (a)	5.43
1982	1,379 (a) (982d)	21,577 (a)	6.39
1983	768 (d)	12,500(g) – 15,500(h)*	6.15
1984	...	11,000(g) – 12,492(i)	...

b. **Kuwaiti exports to Iraq,   1976 – 1984**

	Exports to Iraq	Total Exports	%
1976	68 (b)	9,844 (b)	0.69
1977	47 (b)	9,802 (b)	0.50
1978	88 (b)	10,466 (b)	0.84
1979	227 (b)	18,449 (b)	1.50
1980	420 (b)	20,402 (b)	2.06
1981	1,014 (d)	16,300 (d)	6.22
1982	893 (d)	10,863 (d)	8.22
1983	714 (d)	9,786 (d)	7.30
1984	...	10,569 (d)	...

* sources: see   table I.B.1.a
a. IMF **DTS Yb** 1984
b. id., 1983
c. SAKR, 1982, p. 162: this figure is contradicted by the $ 4.4 m mentioned in UN **Yb ITS 1982,** though it seems to be confirmed by the figure for Kuwaiti exports to Iraq.
d. IMF, **DTS Yb** 1985
* The DTS (1985) figure of 10,415 seems low, and is also strikingly lower than the IFS figure of 12,275.
g. **MEED** estimate (10-8-1985 : 23)
h. E.I.U. est.: EIU, **QER Iraq Anual Supplement 1985,** p. 18
i. See ibid., p. 17

2. KUWAIT TO IRAQ, IN LOCAL CURENCY

a. Iraqi Imports from Kuwait, in ID 1000,   1976 – 1984

	Imports from Kuwait	Total Imports	%	Imp.fr. Arab W.	%
1976	3,879 (a)	1,150,898 (a)	0.34	20,605 (a)	18.83
1977	1,866 (a)	1,323,153 (a)	0.14	22,479 (a)	8.30
1978	3,108 (b)	1,473,575 (b)	0.21	25,005 (b)	12.43
1979	9,312 (b)	1,738,906 (b)	0.54	52,213 (b)	17.83
1980	9,898 (b)	4,208,079 (b)	0.24	69,560 (b)	14.23
1981	...	...		...	
1982	...	...		...	
1983	...	...		...	
1984	...	...		...	

b. Kuwaiti exports to Iraq, in KD 1000,   1976 – 1984

	Exports to Iraq	Total Exports	%	Exp. to Arab W.	%
1976	19,838 (c)	2,874,373 (c)	0.70	232,473 (c)	8.53
1977	13,295 (d)	2,792,631 (d)	0.48	244,060 (d)	5.45
1978	24,039 (d)	2,871,935 (d)	0.84	240,530 (d)	9.99
1979	65,418 (d)	5,088,504 (d)	1.29	382,984 (d)	17.08
1980	113,337 (d)	5,527,279 (d)	2.06	501,827 (d)	22.58
1981	283,232 (d)	4,530,774 (d)	6.26	635,378 (d)	44.58
1982	265,655 (e)(59,300g)	3,128,000 (f)	8.49	583,166 (e)	54.55
				(333,000 g)	(17.81)
1983	... (15,800g)	3,214,000 (f)	2.20*	(198,000 g)	(7.98)
1984	...	...		...	

a. Rep. of Iraq, Min. of Planning. CSO, **Annual Abstract of Statistics 1978.**
b. id. **1981**
c. Kuwait, Min. of Planning, CSO, **Annual Statistical Abstract 1982**
d. id. **1984**
e. Central Bank of Kuwait, Report **1st Quarter 1985**
f. UN **MBS**, Vol. 39, 5, May 1985
g. **MEED**, 20-1-1984, p. 45. Presumably, these figures leave out certain parts of trade, possibly transit trade. In the case of the exports to Arab countries, the **MEED** figures probably count more countries as "Arab".
* Calculated on the assumption that the ratio of the **MEED**-figures to the Kuwaiti ones remains the same as for 1982, i.e. 1 : 4.48.

III. IRAQ – BAHRAIN

A. IRAQ TO BAHRAIN

1. IN US $

a. Iraqi Exports to Bahrain, in US $ millions, 1976 – 1984

	Exports to Bahrain	Total Exports	%
1976	1 (b)	8,518 (b)	0.01
1977	1 (a)	10,372 (a)	0.01
1978	6 (a)	11,979 (a)	0.05
1979	1 (a)	20,320 (a)	0.00
1980	...	28,484 (a)	...
1981	...	11,631 (a)	...
1982	...	10,648 (a)	...
1983	...	8,881 (a)	...
1984	...	...	...

b. Bahraini Imports from Iraq, in US $ 1000,   1976 – 1984

	Imports from Iraq	Total Imports	%
1976	700 (c)	1,664,000 (c)	0.04
1977	456 (d)	2,030,936 (d)	0.02
1978	6,421 (d)	2,032,855 (d)	0.21
1979	1,894 (d)	2,477,504 (d)	0.08
1980	1,158 (d)	3,479,251 (d)	0.03
1981	(471 e *)	4,124,000 (e)	...
1982	...	3,614,100 (e)	...
1983	...	3,342,000 (e)	...
1984	...	...	...

a. IMF **DTS Yb** 1984
b. id. 1983
c. SETRCIC, **Summary Statistics 1980.** One should be wary of comparing these
   figures with the rest: serious discrepancies are sometimes found;
   however, the error in the % is probably not very significant.
d. UN **Yb ITS 1982**
e. UN **MBS,** Vol. 39, 5 (May 1985), and IMF **DTS Yb** 1985
* incomplete (the total 1981-imports figure given in this source is
   $ 1,637,061,000).

2. IRAQ TO BAHRAIN, IN LOCAL CURRENCY

a. Iraqi Exports to Bahrain, in ID 1000, 1976 - 1984

	Exports to Bahrain	Total Exports	%	Exp. to Arab W.	%
1976	350 (a)	2,738,100 (c)	0.01	8,749 (a)	4.00
1977	713 (a)	2,849,600 (c)	0.03	10,734 (a)	6.64
1978	483 (b)	3,266,400 (c)	0.01	15,809 (b)	3.06
1979	1,263 (b)	6,329,000 (c)	0.02	17,267 (b)	7.31
1980	380 (b)	7,760,300 (c)	0.00	10,475 (b)	3.63
1981	...	3,109,700 (c)		...	
1982	...	3,055,700 (c)		...	
1983	...	...		...	
1984	...	...		...	

b. Bahraini Imports from Iraq, in BD 1000, 1976 - 1984

	Imports from Iraq	Total Imports	%	Imp. fr. Arab W.	%
1976	286 (d)	387,644 (d)	0.07	...	
1977	180 (e)	444,853 (e)	0.04	...	
1978	2,486 (f)	453,361 (f)	0.55	...	
1979	...	...		...	
1980	88 (g)	432,011 (g)	0.02	11,866 (g)	0.74
1981	177 (h)	429,607 (h)	0.04	14,393 (h)	1.23
1982	49 (i)	534,426 (i)	0.01	22,067 (i)	0.22
1983	44 (k)	547,342 (k)	0.01	23,057 (k)	0.19
1984	...	...		...	

a. Rep. of Iraq, Min. of Planning, CSO, **Annual Abstract of Statistics 1978**
b. id., **1981**
c. UN **Yb ITS 1982**
d. State of Bahrain, Min. of Fin. and Nat. Econ., **Foreign Trade, 1976**
e. id., **1977**
f. id., **1978**
g. State of Bahrain, CSO, **Statistical Abstract / 1980**
h. id. **1981**
i. id. **1982**
k. id. **1983**

B. BAHRAIN TO IRAQ

1. IN US $

a. Iraqi Imports from Bahrain, in US $ millions

Imports from Bahrain	Total Imports (*)	%
976	4 (b)	3,900	0.10
977	5 (a)	4,481	0.11
978	0.3 (c)	4,212	0.01
979	12 (a)	9,868	0.12
980	...	13,759	
981	...	20,518	
982	...	21,577	
983	...	12,500 - 15,500	
984	...	11,000 - 12,492	

b. Bahraini Exports to Iraq, in US $ 1000,   1976 - 1984

	Exports to Iraq	Total Exports	%
976	4,200 (d)	1,248,200 (d)	0.34
977	10,313 (e)	1,859,408 (e)	0.55
978	6,429 (e)	1,867,204 (e)	0.34
979	2,073 (e)	2,470,529 (e)	0.08
980	20,648 (e)	3,794,815 (e)	0.54
981	33,641 (e)	4,347,000 (f)	0.77
982	...	3,791,000 (f)	
983	...	3,200,000 (f)	
984	...	...	

Sources: see table I.B.1.a.

a. IMF **DTS Yb,** 1984
b. id., 1983
c. SAKR, 1982, p. 162 ("negligible" in a.)
d. SESTRCIC, **Summary Statistics, 1980.** These figures are not compatible
with the others, but the derived % remains equally valid.
e. UN **Yb ITS 1982.** The serious contradiction with the figures for Iraqi
import figures for 1977 to 1979 cannot be explained with the available
data. In fact, it is possible that the $ 12 m which a. has for 1979,
should be situated in 1980.

2. BAHRAIN TO IRAQ, IN LOCAL CURRENCY

a. **Iraqi Imports from Bahrain, in ID 1000, 1976 - 1984**

	Imports fr. Bahrain	Total Imports	%	Imp. fr. Arab W.	%
1976	1,092 (a)	1,150,898 (a)	0.09	20,605 (a)	5.30
1977	1,503 (a)	1,323,153 (a)	0.11	22,479 (a)	6.69
1978	89 (b)	1,473,575 (b)	0.01	25,005 (b)	0.36
1979	1,155 (b)	1,738,906 (b)	0.07	52,213 (b)	2.21
1980	54 (b)	4,208,079 (b)	0.00	69,560 (b)	0.08
1981	...	...		...	
1982	...	...		...	
1983	...	...		...	
1984	...	...		...	

b. **Bahraini Exports to Iraq, in BD 1000, 1976 - 1984**

	Exports to Iraq	Total Exports	%	Exp. to Arab W.	%
1976	1,673 (c)	136,633 (c)	1.22	...	
1977	4,080 (d)	157,606 (d)	2.59	...	
1978	2,192 (e)	147,547 (e)	1.49	...	
1979	...	...		...	
1980	7,781 (f)	39,782 (f)	19.56	17,718 (f)	43.92
1981	12,637 (g)	40,727 (g)	31,03	18,128 (g)	69.71
1982	17,919 (h)	88,317 (h)	20.29	34,830 (h)	51.45
1983	2,706 (i)	115,319 (i)	2.35	21,644 (i)	12.50
1984	...	...		...	

a. Rep. of Iraq, Min. of Planning, CSO, **Annual Abstract of Statistics 1978**
b. id. **1981**
c. State of Bahrain, Min. of Fin. and Nat. Economy, **Foreign Trade, 1976**
d. id., **1977**
e. id., **1978**
f. State of Bahrain, CSO, **Statistical Abstract/ 1980**
g. id., **1981**
h. id., **1982**
i. id., **1983**

IV.   IRAQ   -   UAE

A. IRAQ TO THE UAE

1. IN US $ MILLIONS

a. **Iraqi Exports to the UAE,   1976 - 1984**

	Exports to the UAE	Total Exports	%
1976	3 (1.1 c)	8,518	0.04
1977	1	10,372	0.01
1978	2 (4.1 c)	11,979	0.02
1979	2	20,320	0.01
1980	1	28,484	0.00
1981	5	11,631	0.04
1982	6	10,640	0.06
1983	8	8,652	0.09
1984	...	...	...

b. **UAE Imports from Iraq,   1976 - 1984**

	Imports from Iraq	Total Imports	%
1976	3	3,402	0.09
1977	1	5,186	0.02
1978	2	5,385	0.04
1979	2	6,971	0.03
1980	1	8,597	0.01
1981	6	9,651	0.06
1982	7	10,177	0.07
1983	9	8,356	...
1984	...	7,030	...

Table a: c. UN **Yb ITS 1982.** For 1978, SAKR (1982, p. 162) gives $ 1.5 m.
For   1976,   SESTRCIC,   **Summary   Statistics 1980** gives $ 2.5 m.
The IMF figures therefore seem reliable enough.
1976 : from IMF **DTS Yb** 1983.   1977: from id., 1984.
All others figures from id, 1985.
Table b: 1976 - 1977   : from IMF **DTS Yb** 1983.   All other figures from id.,
1985.

2. IRAQ TO THE UAE, IN LOCAL CURRENCY

a. Iraqi Exports to the UAE, in ID 1000, 1976 - 1984

	Exports to UAE	Total Exports	%	Exp. to Arab W.	%
1976	335 (a)	2,738,100 (c)	0.01	8,749 (a)	3.83
1977	294 (a)	2,849,600 (c)	0.01	10,734 (a)	2.74
1978	1,213 (b)	3,266,400 (c)	0.04	15,809 (b)	7.67
1979	664 (b)	6,329,000 (c)	0.01	17,267 (b)	3.85
1980	517 (b)	7,760,300 (c)	0.01	10,475 (b)	4.94
1981	...	3,109,700 (c)		...	
1982	...	3,055,700 (c)		...	
1983	...	...		...	
1984	...	...		...	

b. UAE Imports from Iraq, in Dh 1000, 1976 - 1984

	Imports from Iraq	Total Imports	%	Imp. fr. Arab W.	%
1976	8,663 (g)	13,430,795 (g)	0.06	859,071 (g)	1.01
1977	2,383 (g)	18,089,685 (g)	0.01	1,216,221 (g)	0.20
1978	...	20,765,000 (f)		...	
1979	...	26,527,000 (f)		...	
1980	6,000 (e)	32,589,100 (e)	0.02	3,348,200 (e)	0.18
1981	21,489 (d)	35,466,600 (e)	0.06	4,480,668 (d)	0.48
1982	26,000 (e)	43,653,600 (e)	0.08	2,780,900 (e)	0.93
1983	...	...		...	
1984	...	...		...	

a. Rep. of Iraq, Min. of Planning, CSO, **Annual Abstract of Statistics 1978.**
b. id., **1981**
c. UN **Yb ITS 1982**
d. UAE, Min. of Planning, **Annual Statistical Abstract 1983**
e. UAE Central Bank, quoted in **MEED, UAE Special Report**, Dec. 1983
f. UN **MBS**, Vol. 39, 5 (May 1985). Figures deviate only slightly from d. and e.
g. UAE, Min. of Planning, **Al-Tijara...**

B.   THE UAE TO IRAQ

1. IN US $ MILLIONS

a. Iraqi Imports from the U.A.E., 1976 - 1984

	Imports from the UAE		Total Imports (*)		%
1976	0.1	(c)	3,900		0.00
1977	...		4,481		
1978	3.9	(d)	4,212		0.09
1979	11	(a)	9,868		0.11
1980	44	(a)	13,759		0.32
1981	85	(a)	20,518		0.41
1982	80	(a)	21,577		0.37
1983	64	(f)	12,500 - 15,500		0.51 - 0.41
1984	...		11,000 - 12,492		...

b. UAE Exports to Iraq,   1976 - 1984

	Exports to Iraq		Total Exports		%
1976	1	(b)	8,591	(b)	0.01
1977	1	(b)	9,637	(b)	0.01
1978	4	(b)	9,125	(b)	0.04
1979	10	(b)	13,652	(b)	0.07
1980	40	(f)	21,618	(f)	0.19
1981	78	(f)	21,238	(f)	0.37
1982	73	(f)	16,837	(f)	0.43
1983	58	(f)	18,765 (f) (15,011 e)		0.31
1984	...		17,636 (f) (14,104 e)		...

* Sources for total exports : see Table I.B.1.a.
a. IMF DTS Yb, 1984
b. id., 1983
c. SESTRCIC, Summary Statistics 1980
d. SAKR, 1982, p. 162
e. IFS Totals, quoted in IMF DTS Yb 1985
f. IMFDTS Yb,1985

2. THE UAE TO IRAQ, IN LOCAL CURRENCY

a. Iraqi Imports from the UAE, in ID 1000,   1976 - 1984

Imports fr. UAE	Total Imports	%	Imp. fr. Arab W.	%
1976	31 (a)	1,150,898 (a)	0.00	20,605 (a)	0.15
1977	14 (a)	1,323,153 (a)	0.00	22,479 (a)	0.06
1978	61 (b)	1,473,575 (b)	0.00	25,005 (b)	0.24
1979	1,190 (b)	1,738,906 (b)	0.07	52,213 (b)	2.78
1980	1,964 (b)	4,208,079 (b)	0.05	69.560 (b)	2.82
1981	...	...		...	
1982	...	...		...	
1983	...	...		...	
1984	...	...		...	

b. UAE non-oil Exports to Iraq, in Dh 1000,   1976 - 1984

non-oil exp. to Iraq	Total n-o Exp.	%	n-o Exp. to Arab W.	%
1976	...	...		...	
1977	...	...		...	
1978	15,322	1,905,674	0.80	...	
1979	39,664	2,944,666	1.35	...	
1980	147,485	4,740,932	3.11	...	
1981	284,616	5,431,760	5.24	...	
1982	266,093	5,040,661	5.28	...	
1983	...	...		...	
1984	...	...		...	

a. Iraq, Min. of Planning, CSO, **Annual Abstract of Statistics 1978**
b. id. **1981**

Table b: all figures from UAE Central Bank,   quoted in **MEED, UAE Special Report**, Dec. 1983. (Including re-exports).

V.   IRAQ - QATAR

A. IRAQ TO QATAR

1. IN US $ MILLIONS

a. Iraqi Exports to Qatar, 1976 - 1984

	Exports to Qatar	Total Exports	%
1976	0.2 (c)	8,518 (b)	0.00
1977	...	10,372 (a)	
1978	1 (a)	11,979 (a)	0.01
1979	-	20,320 (a)	0.00
1980	2 (a)	28,484 (a)	0.01
1981	...	11,631 (a)	
1982	...	10,649 (d)	
1983	...	8,652 (d)	
1984	...	9,681 (d)	

b. Qatari Imports from Iraq, 1976 - 1984

	Imports from Iraq	Total Imports	%
1976	0.2	817.0	0.02
1977	0.4	1,225.1	0.03
1978	0.9	1,183.9	0.08
1979	...	1,425.2	...
1980	1.7	1,439.8	0.12
1981	0.2	1,517.8	0.01
1982	...	1,947.1	...
1983	...	1,455.7	...
1984	...	1,444.8	...

a. IMF **DTS Yb** 1984
b. id. 1983
c. SESTRCIC, **Summary Statistics 1980**
d. IMF **DTS Yb,** 1985

Table b: 1976 - 1979: IMF **DTS Yb,** 1983; 1980 - 1984 : id., 1985.

2. IRAQ TO QATAR, IN LOCAL CURRENCY

a. **Iraqi Exports to Qatar, in ID 1000,   1976 - 1984**

Exports to Qatar	Total exports	%	Exp. to Arab W.	%
1976	140 (a)	2,738,100 (c)	0.01	8,749 (a)	1.60
1977	185 (a)	2,849,600 (c)	0.00	10,734 (a)	1.72
1978	887 (b)	3,266,400 (c)	0.03	15,809 (b)	5.61
1979	268 (b)	6,329,000 (c)	0.00	17,267 (b)	1.55
1980	379 (b)	7,760,300 (c)	0.00	10,475 (b)	3.62
1981	...	3,109,700 (c)		...	
1982	...	3,055,700 (c)		...	
1983	...	...		...	
1984	...	...		...	

b. **Qatari Imports from Iraq, in QR 1000,   1976 - 1984**

Imports from Iraq	Total Imports	%	Imp. fr. Arab W.	%
1976	...	...		...	
1977	1,488 (h)	4,850,095 (h)	0.03	...	
1978	3,626 (h)	4,589,723 (h)	0.08	...	
1979	2,341 (h)	5,377,700 (h)	0.04	...	
1980	6,257 (h)	5,267,922 (g)	0.12	...	
1981	732 (d)	5,524,891 (g)	0.01	...	
1982	207 (e)	7,087,505 (g)	0.00	...	
1983	446 (f)	5,298,642 (g)	0.01	...	
1984	...	...		...	

a. Rep. of Iraq, Min. of Planning, CSO, **Annual Abstract of Statistics 1978**
b. id. **1981.** The 1980 figure for exports to Qatar seems low.
c. UN **Yb ITS 1982**
d. Qatar, CSO, **Foreign Trade Statistics 1981.** (Imports)
e. id. **1982**
f. id.,**1983**
g. Qatar, CSO, **Annual Statistical Abstract,** July 1984
h. Qatar, Customs Department, Statistics Section, **Yearly Bulletin of Imports and Exports for 1980**

QATAR TO IRAQ

1. IN   US $

a. **Iraqi Imports from Qatar,   1976 - 1984 , in US $ millions**

	Imports from Qatar	Total Imports (*)	%
1976	—	3,900	
1977	—	4,481	
1978	—	4,212	
1979	1 (d)	9,868	0.01
1980	25 (d)	13,759	0.18
1981	—	20,518	
1982	—	21,577	
1983	...	12,500 - 15,500	
1984	...	11,000 - 12,492	

b. **Qatari Exports to Iraq,   1976 - 1984,   in US $ 1000**

	Exports to Iraq	Total Exports	%
1976	...	...	
1977	—	2,104,168 (c)	
1978	—	2,367,862 (c)	
1979	536 (c)	3,598,048 (c)	0.01
1980	22,780 (c)	5,310,939 (c)	0.43
1981	...	5,389,121 (c)	
1982	...	4,544,000 (d)	
1983	...	3,616,100 (d)	
1984	...	4,579,500 (d)	

* Sources :see I.B.1.a.
c. UN **Yb ITS 1982**
d. IMF **DTS Yb,** 1985

2. QATAR TO IRAQ, IN LOCAL CURRENCY

a. Iraqi imports from Qatar, 1976 - 1984, in ID 1000

Imports fr. Qatar	Total Imports	%	Imp. fr. Arab W.	%
1976	6 (a)	1,150,898 (a)	0.00	20,605 (a)	0.03
1977	6 (a)	1,323,153 (a)	0.00	22,479 (a)	0.03
1978	2 (b)	1,473,575 (b)	0.00	25,005 (b)	0.00
1979	102 (b)	1,738,906 (b)	0.01	52,213 (b)	0.20
1980	121 (b)	4,208,079 (b)	0.00	69,560 (b)	0.17
1981	...	...		...	
1982	...	...		...	
1983	...	...		...	
1984	...	...		...	

b. Qatari exports to Iraq, in QR

n.a.

QASCO steel exports to Iraq: 1979:   QR   2,017,000
                             1980:   QR 65,670,000
                                                (c)

a. **Rep. of Iraq, Min. of Planning, CSO, Annual Abstract of Statistics 1978**
b. id., **1981**
c. Qatar, Customs Department, Statistics Section, **Yearly Bulletin of imports and Exports for 1980** (no similar rise in exports to any of the other Gulf states, although in absolute terms the rise is equalled by that of steel exports to the UAE: from 66,434 to 130,936).

VI.   IRAQ   -   OMAN

A. IRAQ TO OMAN

1. IN US $ MILLIONS

a. Iraqi Exports to Oman, 1976 - 1984

	Exports to Oman	Total Exports	%
	n		
1976	e - (b,d)	8,518 (b)	0.00
1977	g ...	10,372 (a)	
1978	l - (a,c)	11,979 (a)	0.00
1979	i ...	20,320 (a)	
1980	g...	28,484 (a)	
1981	i..	11,631 (a)	
1982	.b.	10,649 (a)	
1983	..l	8,881 (a)	
1984	...e	...	

b. Omani Imports from Iraq, 1976 - 1984

1976	-	
1977	-	
1978	-	947.3
1979	-	1,246.5
1980	-	1,732.0
1981	-	2,288.2
1982	-	2.682,5
1983	0.1	2,492.3
1984	-	2,748.2

table a:
a. IMF DTS Yb 1984
b. id. 1983
c. SAKR, 1982, p. 162
d. SESTRCIC, Summary Statistics 1980

table b : IMF DTS Yb, 1985

2. IRAQ TO OMAN, IN LOCAL CURRENCY

a. Iraqi Exports to Oman,   1976 - 1984, in ID 1000

	Exports to Oman	Total Exports	%	Exp. to Arab W.	%
1976	- (a)	2,738,100 (c)	0.00	8,749 (a)	0.00
1977	3 (a)	2,849,600 (c)	0.00	10,734 (a)	0.03
1978	- (b)	3,266,400 (c)	0.00	15,809 (b)	0.00
1979	3 (b)	6,329,000 (c)	0.00	17,267 (b)	0.02
1980	1 (b)	7,760,300 (c)	0.00	10,475 (b)	0.01
1981	...	3,109,700 (c)		...	
1982	...	3,055,700 (c)		...	
1983	...	...		...	

b. Omani Imports from Iraq,   1976 - 1984,   in RO 1000

	Imports fr. Iraq	Total Imports	%	Imp. fr. Arab W.	%
1976	- (d)	230,501 (d)	0.00	...	
1977	0.3 (d)	302,064 (d)	0.00	...	
1978	0.1 (d)	372,221 (d)	0.00	...	
1979	2.6 (d)	430,517 (d)	0.00	...	
1980	1.0 (e)	598,245 (d)	0.00	...	
1981	3.9 (e)	790,346 (e)	0.00	...	
1982	- (e)	926,546 (e)	0.00	...	
1983	40.6 (e)	860,852 (e)	0.00	...	
1984	- (e)	949,217 (e)	0.00	...	

a. Rep. of Iraq, Min. of Planning, CSO, **Annual Abstract of Statistics 1978**
b. **id.** 1981
c. **UN** Yb ITS 1982
d. **Oman, D.G. of Customs,** Foreign Trade Statistics 1980
e. **id.** 1984

B. OMAN TO IRAQ

1. IN US $ MILLIONS

a. **Iraqi Imports from Oman, 1976 - 1984**

	Imports from Oman	Total Imports (*)	%
1976	3 (b)	3,900	0.08
1977	4 (a)	4,481	0.09
1978	1 (a)	4,212	0.02
1979	- (d)	9,868	0.00
1980	- (a)	13,759	0.00
1981	- (a)	20,518	0.00
1982	1 (a)	21,577	0.00
1983	1 (k)	12,500 - 15,500	0.00
1984	...	11,000 - 12,492	...

b. **Omani Exports to Iraq, 1976 - 1984**

	Exports to Iraq	Total Exports	%
1976	- (c)	...	0.00
1977	...	1,585 (e)	...
1978	...	1,598 (f)	...
1979	0.02 (d)	2,280 (f,d)	0.00
1980	0.4 (k)	3,294 (k)	0.01
1981	0.3 (k)	4,448 (k)	0.01
1982	1.1 (k)	4,115 (k)	0.03
1983	0.9 (k)	4,051 (k)	0.02
1984	...	3,731 (k)	...

* Sources : see I.B.1.a.
a. IMF **DTS Yb** 1984
b. id. , 1983
c. SESTRCIC, **Summary Statistics 1980**
d. UN **Yb ITS 1982**
e. UN **MBS,** Vol. 39, 6 (June 1985)
f. id., 5 (May 1985)
k. IMF **DTS Yb,** 1985

2. OMAN TO IRAQ, IN LOCAL CURRENCY

a. Iraqi Imports from Oman, 1976 - 1984,   in ID 1000

	Imports from Oman	Total Imports	%	Imp. fr. Arab W.	%
1976	986 (a)	1,150,898 (a)	0.09	20,605 (a)	4.79
1977	1,141 (a)	1,323,153 (a)	0.09	22,479 (a)	5.06
1978	483 (b)	1,473,575 (b)	0.03	25,005 (b)	1.93
1979	1,117 (b)	1,738,906 (b)	0.06	52,213 (b)	2.14
1980	135 (b)	4,208,079 (b)	0.00	69,560 (b)	0.19
1981	...	...		...	
1982	...	...		...	
1983	...	...		...	
1984	...	...		...	

b. Omani non-oil Exports to Iraq, 1976 - 1984,   in RO 1000

	non-oil Exp. to Iraq	Total n-o Exports	%	n-o Exp. to Arab W.	%
1976	...	...		...	
1977	...	...		...	
1978	69 (a)	30,228 (a)	0.23	...	
1979	6 (a)	41,744 (a)	0.01	...	
1980	1,391 (a)	49,856 (a)	2.79	...	
1981	1,110 (b)	95,507 (b)	1.16	...	
1982	3,847 (b)	117,258 (b)	3.28	...	
1983	1,067 (b)	120,716 (b)	0.88	...	
1984	412 (b)	126,619 (b)	0.33	...	

a. Iraq, Min. of Planning, CSO, **Annual Abstract of Statistics 1978**
b. id., **1981**
c. Oman, D.G. of Customs, **Foreign Trade Statistics 1980**
d. id., **1984**

APPENDIX   V
TABLES ON NATIONAL ACCOUNTS AND FINANCIAL SITUATION OF IRAQ AND THE ARAB GULF STATES

TABLE 1. Iraq's financing gap 1980 - 1986, in $ bn, Author's estimates (1)

		Low Case		High Case	
1981	from 22-9				
	War Cost	- 3.0		- 3.0	
	Reserves		+ 35.0		+ 32.0
	Current Account		+ 3.0		+ 2.5
1981	War Cost	- 8.0		- 10.0	
	Current Account	- 12.2		- 13.0	
1982	War Cost	- 11.0		- 12.0	
	Current Account	- 16.0		- 18.0	
1983	War Cost	- 5.5		- 7.0	
	Current Account	- 6.5		- 8.0	
1984	War Cost	- 5.0		- 7.0	
	Current Account	- 3.0		- 4.0	
1985	War Cost	- 5.0		- 7.0	
	Current Account	- 3.0		- 4.0	
Totals		- 78.2	+ 38.0	- 93.0	+ 34.5
FINANCING GAP END-1985		- 40.2		- 58.5	
1986	War Cost	- 8.0		- 10.0	
	Current Account	- 7.0		- 9.0	
Proj. Fin. gap end-1986		- 55.2		- 77.5	
1980-1985:					
Debt to credit agencies of OECD countries			9.2*		9.2*
Debt to companies of OECD countries			6.0*		6.0*
Maintained Reserves		1.0		5.0	
Oil-swaps Saudi Arabia & Kuwait			9.0		9.0
REMAINING GAP END-1985		- 17.0		- 39.3	

(1) based on data from banking sources; **MEED**; **MEES**; **FT**; EIU; IMF;
    Central Bank of Iraq; WHARTON Middle East Economic Service: **FOCI**;
    OECD.
*   **MEED**, 29-3-1986.

TABLE 2.   OIL EXPORTS AND REVENUES OF THE GULF STATES (INCL. IRAN, EXCL. OMAN), 1979-1985

	79	80	81	82	83	84	85
	Net exports (a) mbd						
Saudi Arabia*	9.2	9.6	9.8	6.3	4.3	4.2	2.9
UAE	1.8	1.7	1.5	1.3	1.2	1.2	1.2
Kuwait*	2.5	1.6	1.1	0.9	1.0	1.1	0.9
Iraq	3.3	2.4	0.7	0.7	0.9	0.9	1.2
Iran	2.6	1.1	0.8	1.6	1.7	1.4	1.5
Qatar	0.5	0.5	0.4	0.4	0.3	0.4	0.3
	Oil Revenues in US $ bn.						
Saudi Arabia*	57.5	102.0	113.2	76.0	46.1	43.7	28.0
UAE	12.9	19.5	18.7	16.0	12.8	13.0	12.0
Kuwait*	16.7	17.9	14.9	10.0	9.9	10.8	9.0
Iraq	21.3	26.0	10.4	9.5	8.4	10.4	12.0
Iran	19.1	13.5	8.6	19.0	20.0	15.0	14.0
Qatar	3.6	5.4	5.3	4.2	3.0	4.4	3.0

Source: PE, June 1986, p. 211.
(a) Crude Oil, products and NGL.
*   incl. half of the Divided (Neutral) Zone.

TABLE 3.   SAUDI ARABIA'S CURRENT ACCOUNT SITUATION 1977-1984, IN SDR BN.
(BEFORE SAMA REVISION -   IMF FIGURES)

	1977	1978	1979	1980	1981	1982	1983	1984
Exports fob	34.6	29.5	45.0	77.4	94.2	66.2	42.7	36.5
Imports fob	-12.6	-16.0	-18.2	-21.7	-25.3	-31.2	-31.1	-27.9
Trade bal.	22.0	13.6	26.8	55.7	68.9	35.0	11.7	8.6
Other goods, services and income (+)	5.2	5.2	6.0	8.7	13.8	17.2	19.9	17.2
Id. (-)	-12.3	-15.1	-18.8	-25.2	-41.8	-48.3	-41.9	-44.1
Private unrequited transfers	-1.3	-2.8	-2.6	-3.1	-3.5	-4.8	-5.0	-5.2
Official unreq. transfers	-3.3	-3.1	-2.7	-4.2	-4.8	...	...	...
Curr. Acc.	**10.3**	**-1.8**	**8.6**	**31.8**	**32.5**	**-0.9**	**-15.2**	**-23.5**

Source: IMF, Balance of Payments Statistics, Vol. 36, 1985, p. 537.

TABLE 4.   SAUDI ARABIA: BALANCE OF PAYMENTS FIGURES 1981-1984 (SR MN)
(PRE- AND POST-REVISION)

Trade Surplus		Services & Transf. deficit		Curr. Acc. Balance	
Pre	Post	Pre	Post	Pre	Post
1981					
274,761	277,174	145,035	132,532	+ 129,726	+ 144,642
1982					
132,480	135,175	136,247	109,220	- 3,599	+ 25,955
1983					
43,064	43,110	99,339	98,616	- 56,275	- 55,995
1984					
31,113	31,343	115,814	98,451	- 84,701	- 56,275

Source: **MEED**, 17-5-1986.

TABLE 5.   SAUDI RESERVES, 1979-1984, IN $ BN, ACCORDING TO IMF FIGURES

	1979	1980	1981	1982	1983	1984
Exch. rate (SR per $, market rate end of period)						
	3.3650	3.3250	3.4150	3.4350	3.4950	3.6450
"Total Reserves" minus gold (Liquid: SDRs, IMF reserve pos., For. exch.)						
	19.27	23.44	32.24	29.55	27.29	24.75
Gold	4.57	4.57	4.57	4.57	4.57	4.57
SAMA						
Foreign Assets	61.65	87.44	128.81	128.81	140.97	132.62
Reserve Money	11.37	10.33	11.48	13.00	12.51	12.03
Gov't deposits	32.80	55.67	114.83	100.20	94.24	80.81
Other items (net)	17.35	21.41	20.95	27.78	25.86	25.07
Total	123.17	174.85	276.07	281.95	265.23	235.82

Calculated on the basis of data in SR mn, in **IFS**, May 1986.

**TABLE 6.   SAMA'S INTEREST-EARNING FOREIGN ASSETS IN 1983-1984, IN $ BN,
ACCORDING TO** INSTITUTIONAL INVESTOR'S **ARTICLE BY MUEHRING,1984**

		APRIL 1983	AUGUST 1984
US $	TOTAL	**76.5**	**56.5**
	Government Securities	48.0	37.3
	Bank Deposits	21.3	12.7
	Corporate Stocks & Bonds	7.2	6.5
DM	TOTAL	**11.9**	**11.5**
	Government Securities	10.5	10.0
	Other	1.4	1.5
YEN	TOTAL	**12.2**	**11.5**
	Government Securities	10.8	...
	Other	1.4	...
OTHER,TOTAL		**13.6**	**12.5**
	Government Securities	11.8	...
	Other	1.7	...
SDRs		**4.0**	**8.5**
GRAND TOTAL		**118.2**	**100.5**

Source: MUEHRING, 1984.

TABLE 7.   KUWAIT,   CURRENT ACCOUNT SITUATION 1977-1984, IN SDR BN

	1977	1978	1979	1980	1981	1982	1983	1984
Exports fob	8.2	8.2	14.0	15.9	13.6	9.8	10.6	11.8
Imports fob	-4.1	-3.5	-3.8	-5.2	-5.7	-7.1	-6.5	-7.1
Trade bal.	4.1	4.7	10.2	10.7	7.9	2.7	4.1	4.7
Other goods, services & income (+)	2.2	2.9	3.7	5.2	8.3	6.9	6.2	6.5
Id. (-)	-1.4	-1.7	-2.1	-2.8	-3.1	-3.8	-4.0	-4.5
Private unrequited transfers	-0.3	-0.3	-0.4	-0.5	-0.5	-0.8	-0.8	-0.8
Official unreq. transfers	-0.8	-0.6	-0.6	-0.6	-0.8	-0.6	-0.6	-0.4
Curr. Acc.	**3.9**	**4.9**	**10.9**	**11.8**	**11.7**	**4.4**	**4.8**	**5.4**

Source: IMF, **Balance of Payments Statistics**, Vol. 36, 1985, p. 351.

TABLE 8.   KUWAIT, BALANCE OF PAYMENTS 1983-1986, IN $ MN

	1983	1984	1985 a	1986 b
Exports & re-exports (fob)	11,356	12,058	10,100	9,400
of which petroleum	9,948	10,394	8,400	8,000
Imports (fob)	6,982	7,289	6,270	6,500
Trade surplus	4,374	4,769	3,830	2,000
Services	2,285	2,060	2,000	2,200
Unrequited transfers	-1,544	-1,265	-1,250	-1,250
Current Account Surplus	5,115	5,564	4,580	3,850

Source: IMF,**IFS**, February 1986, as in **MEED**, 15-3-1986.
a: MEED estimate;   b: MEED forecast.

TABLE 9.   KUWAIT: PUBLIC FINANCE, FINANCIAL YEARS 1983-1986, IN $ MN

	1983	1984	1985	1986 a
Revenue	8,855	10,794	9,112	8,000
Investment income	5,717	4,381	3,980 b	4,200
Expenditure	10,895	9,936	10,641	10,000
Overall Surplus	3,677	5,239	2,451	2,200

Source: Central Bank of Kuwait, as in **MEED**, 15-3-1986.
a: MEED forecast;   b: MEED estimate.

TABLE 10.   KUWAITI RESERVES,   1981-1985,   IN KD BN.

	RFFG	SGR	TOTAL	% SGR
31 December 1981	...	...	18.77	...
30 June 1982	7.55	12.40	19.95	62.2
31 December 1982	...	...	20.67	...
30 June 1983	9.38	12.42	21.80	57.0
31 December 1983	...	...	21.98	...
30 June 1984	10.82	11.67	22.58	52.1
31 December 1984	11.51	11.52	23.02	50.0
30 June 1985	11.84	11.43	23.27	49.1
31 December 1985	12.89	11.24	24.13	46.6

Source: **MEES,** 26-5-1986.

APPENDIX   VI
LIST OF THE MAIN JOINT ORGANISATIONS AND VENTURES LINKING IRAQ TO THE
ARAB GULF STATES

A. IN WIDER ARAB FRAMEWORK.

1. **Arab League**   (1945)   Tunis
   Council for Arab Economic Unity   (1964)   Amman
   Economic Commission for Western Asia: ECWA   (1974)   Baghdad
        (since 1985: ESCWA: Economic & Social...)
   Arab Fund for Social and Economic Development (1968/73) Kuwait
   OPEC
   Arab Monetary Fund: AMF   (1977)   Abu Dhabi

2. Iraq is a member of most Arab Specialised Unions and Federations,
   almost half (six) of which are headquartered in Baghdad (the **A.F.**
of Engineering Industries; the **A. F. of paper Industries; A.F. of
Shipping Industries; Arab Seaports Union; A.U. of Fish Producers;
A.U. of Food Industries**).

3. Iraq and most of the Six are members of the Arab Joint Companies:

   Arab Company for Drug Industries and Medical Appliances (ACDIMA)
                                                        Amman
   A.C. for Industrial Investment (ACII)   Baghdad
   A.C. for Livestock Development (ARCOLID)   Damascus
   Arab Mining Company   Amman
   The Arab Investment Company (TAIC)   Riyadh

4. With the other A.L. members, Iraq and the Gulf states belong to
   some fifteen Specialised Agencies, such as the **Arab Academy for
Maritime Transport** (Sharjah); the **Arab Centre for the Study of Arid
and Dry Lands (ACSAD); Arab Industrial Development Organisation
(AIDO)** - thus renamed since 1980 and headquartered in Baghdad); the
Arab Satellite Communications Organisation - under whose auspices
ARABSAT was set up; and, as an important last example, the **Inter-Arab
Investment Guarantee Corporation,** since 1974 headquartered in
Kuwait).

B. OAPEC AND ITS JOINT VENTURES:

   Gulf members of **OAPEC** (1968 - Kuwait) are Iraq, Bahrain, Kuwait,
Qatar and Saudi Arabia (in addition to Algeria, Libya, Syria and
Tunisia).

Arab Engineering Company (AREC)   (1981)   Abu Dhabi
Arab Maritime Petroleum Transport Co. (AMPTC)   (1973)   Kuwait
Arab Petroleum Investment Corporation (APICORP)   (1975)   Dhahran
Arab Petroleum Services Co. (APSC)   (1977)   Tripoli
Arab Petroleum Training Institute   (1979)   Baghdad

Arab Shipbuilding and Repairs Yard (ASRY)   (1974)   Manama
Arab Engineering Consultancy Company   (1981)   Abu Dhabi

C. ARAB REGIONAL DEVELOPMENT INSTITUTIONS.

   In addition to **AFESD**, there are the **Arab Bank for Economic
Development in Africa (ABEDA)**; the **Arab Authority for Agricultural
Investment and Development (AAAID)**; the **Islamic Development Bank,
OPEC Special Fund**, and others.

D. THE GULF AND THE ARABIAN PENINSULA.

1. **Conference of Ministers of Agriculture of the Gulf States and the
   Arabian Peninsula (CMAGSAP).**
   Combines Iraq with the Six and the two Yemens, since 1976.
   Amongst other things initiates joint agricultural projects.

2. **Gulf Organisation for Industrial Consulting (GOIC)** (1976) Doha
   Members: Iraq and the Six.
   Advises on Industrial Investment, and studies and proposes joint
   projects. Its first brainchild to start operations was **GARMCO.**

3. **GARMCO: the Gulf Aluminium Rolling Mill Company** (1981) Bahrain
   Capital subscribed 20 % each by Saudi Arabia, Bahrain, Iraq,
   Kuwait; 10 % each by Qatar and Oman; the UAE has an option to
   join.

4. **GULFERT**, an organisation bringing together the producers of
   chemical fertilisers in the the Gulf, including Iraq and Iran.
   Apparently defunct since the Iranian Revolution.

5. **United Arab Shipping Company (UASC)**   (1976) Kuwait
   Created fromm Kuwait's shipping fleet, its members now are, in
addition to Kuwait, Bahrain, Iraq, Qatar, and the UAE.

6. **Gulf International Bank (GIB)**   (1975) Manama
   Capital subscribed by Iraq and the Six.

7. **Arab War Risks Insurance Syndicate.**

Some examples of joint ventures with mixed / private capital:

8. **Arab Iron and Steel Company**   (1978) Bahrain
   capital from Bahrain, Iraq, Kuwait and the UAE.

9. **Consolidated Gulf Servives and Industries Co.**   (1980) Dubai

10. **Arab International Insurance Co.**   (1980) Manama
    capital contributed by insurance cos. from Iraq and the Gulf,
    excl. Kuwait.

Other joint organisations are situated in the fields of environmental
protection, Education and Information and Culture:

12. **Regional Organisation for the Protection of the Marine
    Environment (ROPME)**   (1978) Kuwait
    Initially included Iran, but in its present form has only Iraq,
    Bahrain, Kuwait, Qatar, and Saudi Arabia as members.

13. **Bureau for Education in the Arab Gulf States**   (1975) Riyadh
    Members: Iraq and the Six.
    Has initiated and overseen the creation of the **Gulf University** in
    Bahrain, in 1981.

14. **Gulf News Agency**   (1976) Manama

15. **Arab Gulf States Joint Programme Production Corporation**
                                                     (1976) Kuwait

16. **Gulf Information Documentation Centre**   (1981) Baghdad

17. **Gulf Popular Heritage Centre**   Doha

18. **Gulf-Vision**   (1976) Riyadh

The latter five all include Iraq and the Six.

This list is not exhaustive; for further examples and details, see
ECWA,   1979; the annual ECWA **Survey of economic and Social
Developments in the ECWA Region,** 1980-1985; the 1980 and 1981 issues
of the ECWA **Studies on Development Problems in countries of Western
Asia;** NONNEMAN, 1981; and SAKR, 1982.

APPENDIX   VII
TEXT OF THE GCC FOREIGN MINISTERS' COMMUNIQUE OF 3 MARCH 1986

The Council discussed the grave situation in the region in the light of Iran' occupation of portions of Iraqi territory, and the breach of international conventions and the principles of good neighbourliness, and violation of Iraq's sovereignty and territorial integrity, which that occupation represents. Condemning that occupation, the Council calls on Iran to withdraw its forces immediately to the international border.

The Council also discussed the threats issued by Iran against member states of the GCC and the consequent expansion of the scope of the conflict. The GCC states have always adhered to relations of good neighbourliness based on mutual respect and non-interference in the international affairs. But the Iranian threats have created a climate of tension. Therefore, the GCC calls on Iran to refrain fom its threats which are helping to shake the security and stability of the region.

The Council recalls the decisions taken by the GCC Heads of State at previous sessions of the GCC Supreme Council, affirming that the preservation of the security and stability of member states is a joint responsibility to be discharged by all the states on the basis of the principles enshrined in the GCC's Charter. Recalling in particular the Summit's decision to establish the 'Peninsula Shield Force' and the tasks entrusted to it, the GCC affirms that this force is ready to move to any location which might be affected by the recent developments. The Chiefs of Staff will meet to take the measures necessary to confront the possible dangers.

On the political level, the Council decided to intensify its contacts with fraternal Arab countries and all states of the world in order to construct an Arab-international position which might help distance the region from the dangers of conflict and eliminate tension from it.

The Council affirms the adherence of its member states to the policy instituted by its Heads of State, of preserving the region's neutrality and resisting any action which could carry the Gulf into the cycle of international rivalry, and of commitment to peaceful coexistence between all states of the region, to non-interference in international affairs, and to the solution of problems by peaceful means.

The GCC also affirms its support for Iraq's readiness to accept a peaceful solution to its war with Iran, and it calls on Iran to abide by the United Nations Resolutions and the eforts of the Islamic Conference Organisation, the Non-Aligned Movement, and a number of states, to achieve a peaceful settlement of the problems between the two countries.

————

Map 1. The Arabian Peninsula, the Gulf, Iraq and the Levant

Taken from BOYD, Andrew, **An Atlas of World Affairs**,
London: Methuen, 1983, p. 123

Map 2. The Gulf

Taken from BOYD, Op. Cit., p. 125

Map 3. The northern Gulf and the Iran-Iraq border

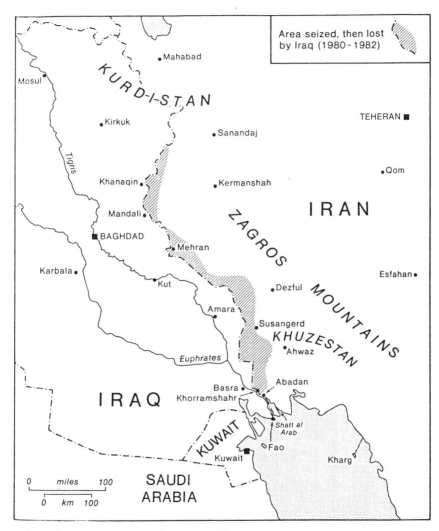

Taken from BOYD, Op. Cit., p. 129

Map 4.   The Shatt al-Arab and the Fao peninsula

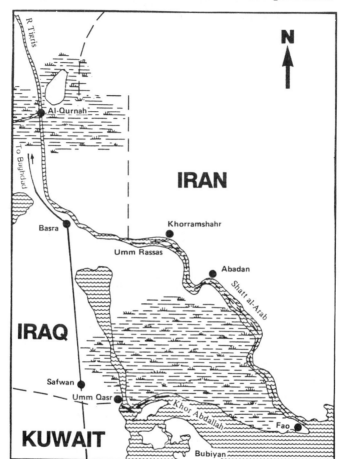

Taken from **MEED**, 22 February 1986, p. 7

BIBLIOGRAPHY

ABBREVIATIONS FOR PERIODICALS AND NEWSPAPERS CONSULTED

AAA   American-Arab Affairs
AER   Al-taqrir al-iqtisadi al-'arabi (annual)
AOG   Arab Oil and Gas
Arabia   Arabia: the Islamic World Review
AR&MEMO   An-Nahar Arab Report & MEMO
AT   Arab Times
BO   Baghdad Observer
BW   Business Week
EN   Emirates News
EIU QER Iraq   Economist Intelligence Unit: Quarterly Economic
                        Report, Iraq
EIU QER Saudi Arabia   id., Saudi Arabia
EIU QER B-Q-O-Y   id., Bahrain, Qatar, Oman and the Yemens
FET   Foreign Economic Trends and Implication for the US
                        (US Department of Commerce)
FT   Financial Times
IHT   International Herald Tribune
IMF DTS Yb   IMF Direction of Trade Statistics Yearbook
KEESING'S   Keesing's Contemporary Archives
KT   Kuwait Times
ME   The Middle East
MEED   Middle East Economic Digest
MEER   Middle East Executive Reporter
MEES   Middle East Economic Survey
MEI   Middle East International
MEJ   Middle East Journal
MEM   MidEast Markets
MERIP   Middle East Research and Information Project - Reports
OPEC NB   OPEC News Bulletin
PE   Petroleum Economist
PIW   Petroleum Intelligence Weekly
ST   Sunday Times
SWB   BBC: Summary of World Broadcasts
UN MBS   United Nations: Monthly Bulletin of Statistics
UN Yb ITS   United Nations: Yearbook of International
                        Trade Statistics
WHARTON FOCI   Wharton Middle East Economic Service: Focus
                        on Current Issues

OTHER PERIODICALS CONSULTED, not abbreviated
(in **bold** if in Arabic):

Akhbar al-Khalij   (Bahrain)
Akhbar al-Yaum   (Egypt)
Alwaqai Aliraqiya. The Official Gazette of the Republic of Iraq
Arab Gulf Journal
Agefi Review
Al-Anbaa'   (Kuwait)
Arab News   (Saudi Arabia)
Arab Shipping
Aswaq al-Khalij
Atlantic Community Quarterly
Al-Bayan   (UAE)
Diyaruna wa-l-'Alam   (Qatar)
The Economist
Foreign Affairs
The Guardian
Gulf Daily News   (Bahrain)
Gulf Mirror   (Bahrain)
Gulf News   (UAE)
Institutional Investor
Internationale Spectator (Netherlands)
Al-Ittihad   (UAE)
Al-Jazira   (Saudi Arabia)
Jordan Times
Journal of the Arab Gulf   (**Majallat al-Khalij al-'Arabi**)
Khaleej Times   (UAE)
Al-Madina   (Saudi Arabia)
Middle East Newsletter, Saudi Arabia
Middle East Reporter
Middle East Review (annual)
Al-Musawwar   (Egypt)
An-Nadwa   (Saudi Arabia)
An-Nahar   (Lebanon)
The Observer
Orient (Opladen)
Al-Qabas   (Kuwait)
Al-Ra'y al-'Amm   (Kuwait)
Al-Riyadh   (Saudi Arabia)
Saudi Gazette
Al-Sharq al-Awsat   (Saudi Arabia)
Al-Siyasa   (Kuwait)
De Standaard   (Belgium)
Strategy Week
Time (Europe)
The Times
VVN-Berichten   (Belgium)

Wall Street Journal
Al-Watan   (Kuwait)
Al-Watan al-'Arabi   (Paris)
World Today

— — — — —

BOOKS AND ARTICLES

ABDUL RAZZAK, Sufyan
        1982   Die Interessen- und Konfliktkonstellationen in der
                Arabische Golf-Region.
                Hamburg: Borg.

AFESD (=Arab Fund for Economic and Social Development), Coordination
Secretariat
        1985   Financing Operations. Arab National and Regional
                Development Institutions. Summary of Sectors.
                December 31, 1984.   Kuwait: AFESD.

AHMAD, Ahmad Yousef
        1984   'The Dialectics of Domestic Environment and Role Perform-
                ance : The Foreign Policy of Iraq'.
                in: KORANY, B. and DESSOUKI, A.E.H. (eds.), The Foreign
                Policies of Arab States.
                Boulder/London/Cairo: Westview/AUCP.   pp. 147-173.

AMERICAN EMBASSY BAGHDAD
        1985   Iraq   (= FET 85-48, June 1985)
                Washington: US Dep't of Commerce.

AMIN, S.H.
        1984   Political and Strategic Issues in the Persian-Arabian Gulf.
                Glasgow: Royston Ltd.

AMOS, John W., II
        1984   'The Iraq-Iran War: Conflict, Linkage, and Spillover in the
                Middle East', in: DARIUS, AMOS,II, and MAGNUS (eds.), Gulf
                Security into the 1980s.
                Stanford : Hoover Institution Press. pp.49-81.

ANTHONY, John Duke
        1982   'Aspects of Saudi Arabia's relations with other Gulf

                    States', in: NIBLOCK, T. (ed.), State, Society and Economy
                    in Saudi Arabia.   London: Croom Helm.   pp. 148-170.

AXELGARD, Fred
        1985   'Iraq and the Gulf War'. Unpublished paper.

_____ 1986   Iraq in Transition. A political, Economic and
                    Strategic Perspective.
                    Boulder, Col./London: Westview Press / Mansell Publ.

AYUBI, Nazih N. M.
        1983   'Arab Relations in the Gulf: the Future and its
                    Prologue', in: TAHIR-KHELI and AYUBI (eds.), The Iran-
                    Iraq War.
                    New York: Praeger.   pp. 146-171.

AZHARY, M.S. El- (ed.)
        1984   The Iran - Iraq War.   London: Croom Helm.

BRAUN, Ursula
        1981   'Die Aussen- und Sicherheitspolitik Saudi Arabiens',
                    in: **Orient** (Opladen), 22, pp. 219-240.

CORDESMAN, Anthony H.
        1984   The Gulf and the Search for Strategic Stability.
                    Boulder/London : Westview/ Mansell.

DAWISHA, Adeed I.
        1980   'Iraq: The West's Opportunity'
                    in: **Foreign Policy**, Vol. 41, pp. 134-153.

_____ 1981a   'Iraq and the Arab World: the Gulf War and after',
                    in: **World Today**, 37, pp. 188-194.

_____ 1981b   'The Impact of the Gulf War on Arab Politics',
                    in: Der Iranisch-Irakische Konflikt. Ein Krieg ohne
                    Gewinner. (=Analysen aus der Abteilung Entwicklungs-
                    laenderforschung, 98/99).
                    Bonn: Forschungsinstitut der Friedrich Ebert Stiftung,
                    pp. 55-67.

_____ 1983 (ed.)
                    Islam in Foreign Policy.
                    Cambridge: Cambridge University Press.

ECWA-Development Planning Division   .
        1979   Evolution of Economic Cooperation and Integration in
                    Western Asia.   s.l. (Beirut).

FAROUK-SLUGLETT, Marion & SLUGLETT, Peter
        1984   'Not quite Armageddon: Impact of the War on Iraq',

              in: **MERIP**, July-September, pp. 22-30.

_____   1985   'From Gang to Elite: The Iraqi Baath Party's
                  Consolidation of Power'.   Unpublished paper,
                  presented at the IPSA annual Conference, Paris, 15-20
                  July 1985.

GHAREEB, Edmund
       1983   'The Forgotten War', in: **AAA**, 5, pp. 59-75.

_____   1986   'Iraq in the Gulf', in: AXELGARD (ed.), 1986,
                  pp. 59-83.

GOIC (Gulf Organisation for Industrial Consulting)
       1979   Petrochemical Marketing Strategies for the Arab Gulf
              States in the 1980s.   Doha.

HEARD-BEY, Frauke
       1983   Die Arabische Golfstaaten im Zeichen der islamischen
              Revolution.   (= Arbeitspapiere zur internationalen
              Politik, 25).   Bonn: Forschungsinstitut der Deutschen
              Gesellschaft fuer Auswaertige Politik e.V.

HELLER, Mark
       1984   The Iran-Iraq War: Implications for third parties.
              (= JCSS paper no. 23, January).
              Tel Aviv: Jaffee Center for Strategic Studies.

HELMS, Christine Moss
       1983   'The Iraqi Dilemma' in: **AAA**, 5, pp. 76-85.

_____   1984   Iraq, Eastern Flank of the Arab World.
                  Washington: the Brookings Institution.

HIRO, Dilip
       1984   'Chronicle of the Gulf War', in: **MERIP**, July-September,
              pp. 3-14.

HIZB AL-BA'TH AL-'ARABI AL-ISHTIRAKI (al-Qutr al-'Iraqi)
       1983   Al-Taqrir al-Markazi li-l-Mu'tamar al-Qutri
              al-Tasi'. Haziran 1982.
              Baghdad: Tab' al-Dar al-'Arabiya.

HUSSEIN, Saddam
       1979   On Social and Foreign Affairs in Iraq.
              London: Croom Helm.

HUSSAIN, Saddam
       1981   Al-'Iraq wa-l-Siyasa al-Duwaliya.
              Baghdad: Dar al-Hurriya li-l-Taba'a.

ISKANDER, Amir
        1980   Saddam Hussein. Le militant, le penseur et l'homme.
                    Paris: Hachette.

JANSEN, G.H.
        1984   'The attitudes of the Arab Governments',
                    in: AZHARY, 1984,   pp. 81-87.

KASHKETT, S.B.
        1982   'Iraq and the pursuit of non-alignment',
                    in: Orbis, 26 (Summer),   pp. 477-494.

KHAFAJI, Al-
        1984   Al-Dawla wa-l-Tatawwur al-Ra'smali fi-l-'Iraq.
                    Cairo.

KORANY, Baghat & DESSOUKI, Ali E. Hillal
        1984   The Foreign Policies of Arab States.
                    Boulder, Col.:   Westview Press (with AUCP).

LITWAK, Robert
        1981   Security in the Persian Gulf, 2. Sources of Inter-
                    State Conflict.
                    Aldershot: Gower, for IISS.

LLOYDS BANKING GROUP
        1985   Economic Report 1985: Iraq.   London: Lloyds B.G.

MARTIN. Lenore G.
        1984   The Unstable Gulf. Threats from within.
                    Lexington, Mass.: D.C. Heath & Co.

MUEHRING, Kevin
        1984   'Inside SAMA', in: Institutional Investor, November,
                    pp. 61-86.

MUGHISUDDIN, Mohammed
        1977   'Iraqi Foreign Policy', in: McLAURIN, MUGHISUDDIN,
                    WAGNER, Foreign Policy Making in the Middle East.
                    New York : Praeger. pp. 108-168.

NATIONAL WESTMINSTER BANK
        1985   Iraq. An economic report. (May).

NIBLOCK, Tim
        1980   'The prospects for Integration in the Arab Gulf',
                    in: NIBLOCK (ed.), Social and Economic Development in
                    the Arab Gulf.
                    London: Croom Helm.   pp. 187-209.
_____ 1982   'Iraqi Policies towards the Arab States of the Gulf,
                    1958-1981'.

in: NIBLOCK (ed.), Iraq: The Contemporary State.
London: Croom Helm.   pp. 125-149.

NOBLE, Paul C.
    1984   'The Arab System: Opportunities, Constraints and
            Pressures',   in: BAGHAT & KORANY (EDS.), 1984, pp.
            41-77.

NONNEMAN, Gerd
    1981   Regionale integratie in de Arabische Golf.
            Unpublished 'Licentiate's' thesis at Gent University
            - ISVO - (Belgium).

_____ 1984a   'De Golfoorlog tussen Iran en Iraq',
            in: **VVN-Berichten**, no. 41 (May-June), pp. 33-52.

_____ 1984b   'De Golfoorlog: achtergronden en perspectieven',
            in: **Internationale Spectator**, September (Vol. 38, no.
            9), pp. 554-564, 553.

OMAIR, Ali Abdulaziz al-
    1979   The Arabian Gulf: a study of stability and integration
            in the realm of regional and international politics
            after British withdrawal in 1971.
            Unpublished PhD. thesis - mimeographed (Ann Arbor).

OTAQUI, Shakib
    1985   'Kuwait', in: **Middle East Review**, 1985, pp. 125-137.

PETERSON, John E.
    1983   'The Arab Response to the Iranian Challenge in the
            Gulf', in: STODDARD, Philip H.(ed.),   The Middle East
            in the 1980s: Problems and Prospects.
            s.l.(Middle East Institute and the Defence Intelli-
            gence College).   pp. 153-164.

PISCATORI, James P.
    1983   'Islamic Values and National Interest: the Foreign
            Policy of Saudi Arabia', in: DAWISHA (ed.), 1983,
            pp. 33-53.

QUANDT, William B.
    1981   Saudi Arabia in the 1980s. Foreign Policy, Security
            and Oil.
            Washington: the Brookings Institution.

_____ 1981b   'Reactions of the Arab Gulf States', in: DESSOUKI,
            A.E.H. (ed.), The Iran-Iraq War. Issues of Con-
            flict and Prospects for Settlement (Proceedings of
            a seminar).
            Princeton: Centre for International Studies / Woodrow

Wilson School for Public and International Affairs.
pp. 39-46.

_____   1984   'The Gulf War: Policy Options and Regional Implications', in: **AAA**, 9, pp. 1-7.

THE 1968 REVOLUTION IN IRAQ. Experience and Progress. The Political
1979   Report of the Eighth Congress of the Arab Ba'th Socialist Party in Iraq, January 1974.
London: Ithaca Press.

SAFRAN, Nadav
1985   Saudi Arabia. The Ceaseless Quest for Security.
Cambridge, Mass.: The Belknap Press of Harvard University Press.

SAKR, Naomi
1982   'Economic Relations between Iraq and other Arab Gulf
States', in: NIBLOCK (ed), Iraq: The Contemporary
State.
London: Croom Helm.   pp. 150-167.

SALAMEH, Ghassan
1984   'Checkmate in the Gulf War', in: **MERIP**, July-
September, pp. 15-21.

SPRINGBORG, Robert
1985   'Infitah, Agrarian Transformation, and Elite Consoli-
dation in Contemporary Iraq"
Unpublished paper presented to the International P.S.A.
annual conference, Paris, 15-20 July.

STAUDENMAIER, William o.
1983   ´The Iran-Iraq War:ₐ 'A Strategic Analysis',
in: TAHIR-KHELI & AYUBI (eds.), The Iran-Iraq War.
New York: Praeger.   pp. 27-50.

STORK, Joe and WENGER, Martha
1984   'US ready to Intervene in Gulf War',
in: **MERIP**, July-September, pp. 44-48.

TINNIN, D.T.
1981   'Iraq and the new Arab Alliance', in: **Atlantic
Community Quarterly**, 18 (Winter '80-'81), pp. 473-478.

UAE, MINISTRY OF PLANNING
s.d.   Al-Tijara al-Kharijiya wa-l-Mizan al-Tijari fi Dawlat
al-Imarat al-'Arabiya al-Muttahida 1975 - 1979.
Abu Dhabi.

WAQA'I' AL-MU'TAMAR AL-SUHUFI li-l-Ra'is Saddam Hussain
        1985   ma'a-l-suhufiyin al-Masriyin fi 20-7-1985.
                London: Iraqi Embassy.

WHARTON MIDLE EAST ECONOMIC SERVICE
        1985   Middle East Economic Outlook, April 1985.

WRIGHT, Claudia
        1980   'Implications of the Iraq-Iran War',
                in: **Foreign Affairs,** 59 (1980-81), pp. 275-303.

_____ 1983   'Neutral or Neutralized? Iraq, Iran and the Super-
                powers', in: TAHIR-KHELI & AYUBI (eds.), The Iraq-
                Iran War.
                New York: Praeger.   pp. 172-194.

I N D E X
(exclusive of appendices)